NEXT.JS 15 FOR ENTERPRISE APPLICATIONS: ARCHITECTING HIGH-PERFORMANCE WEB SOLUTIONS

Matt P. Handy

TABLE OF CONTENTS

CONTENTS

INTRODUCTION

Welcome to the World of Enterprise Next.js

Hey there, fellow developer! If you're picking up this book, chances are you're facing the exciting challenge of building serious, impactful web applications – the kind that power businesses, connect communities, and handle real-world complexity. You're not just throwing together a quick landing page; you're architecting a solution that needs to be robust, scalable, and performant. That's where Next.js 15 comes in, and that's precisely why I'm so excited to guide you through it.

You might be familiar with Next.js as the darling of the React ecosystem, known for its fantastic developer experience and out-of-the-box features. But in the enterprise world, it's about more than just convenience. It's about creating a stable foundation, about thinking long-term, and about crafting solutions that can grow with your business. And that's where the latest version, Next.js 15, really shines, offering a range of improvements and features specifically geared for the demanding needs of enterprise applications.

This book is your deep dive into using Next.js 15 for just that – building high-performance web solutions that meet the rigor and expectations of enterprise environments. We're not just going to scratch the surface. We'll go beyond the basics, delving into the architectural patterns that make large-scale applications manageable, the performance optimizations that deliver a truly exceptional user experience, and the deployment strategies that ensure seamless operations.

We'll be tackling practical, real-world problems, not just abstract concepts. You'll find working, up-to-date code examples—the kind you can adapt and use directly in your projects. I'll walk you through these examples step-by-step, explaining the "why" behind the code, not just the "how." Think of this book as your trusted companion on the journey, bringing clarity and insight to the often complex process of enterprise application development.

I've personally wrestled with the challenges of building and scaling web applications in various contexts, and I've seen firsthand how powerful Next.js can be when wielded thoughtfully. This book isn't just about a framework; it's about a mindset, a way of approaching software development that emphasizes quality, performance, and sustainable growth.

So, if you're ready to take your Next.js skills to the next level and start architecting the web of the future, then let's jump in. Let's explore how Next.js 15 can be your secret weapon for building exceptional enterprise web applications. Let's start building.

PART 1: FOUNDATIONS FOR ENTERPRISE DEVELOPMENT

CHAPTER 1: NEXT.JS 15 IN THE ENTERPRISE LANDSCAPE

Alright, let's kick things off by exploring why Next.js 15 is making waves in the enterprise world. We'll get a good understanding of what makes an enterprise app tick, why Next.js is a great fit, how to set up your environment, and some hurdles we should anticipate. Think of this as laying the groundwork for your journey into building robust, scalable web solutions.

1.1 UNDERSTANDING ENTERPRISE WEB APPLICATION NEEDS

So, you're embarking on the journey of building something substantial—an *enterprise web application*. It's more than just code on a screen; it's a digital engine that powers businesses, connects users, and manages critical information. But what truly makes these applications different? Let's unpack the key characteristics and needs that define them.

At its core, an enterprise web application is a system designed to solve complex problems within an organization. Think of it as the digital backbone for operations, customer interaction, and data management. These applications are generally characterized by their *scale*, *complexity*, and *critical role* in day-to-day business.

Defining the Enterprise Landscape

Unlike smaller websites or single-purpose web tools, enterprise applications need to be robust, adaptable, and secure. They often handle large volumes of data, support numerous users, and integrate with diverse systems, from CRMs and ERPs to payment gateways and other legacy systems. This level of complexity demands a careful understanding of what we're building.

Key Characteristics of Enterprise Apps

Here are some crucial aspects of an enterprise web application you should keep in mind:

- **Reliability:** This is non-negotiable. Enterprise apps need to operate consistently without unexpected downtime. They have to handle numerous concurrent users and various interactions without crashing. Imagine a financial system failing during month-end closing—it's a nightmare scenario. Reliability isn't just about coding practices; it's also about a well-planned deployment strategy, solid error handling, and robust monitoring.
- **Scalability:** They must be designed to handle increasing loads. A website that works fine for 100 users might struggle with 10,000. Scalability isn't just about handling traffic; it's also about scaling your data storage, server resources, and your development team. A flexible architecture is crucial, allowing you to adapt and add resources as needed.
- **Security:** Data security is paramount. Sensitive information like user data, financial transactions, and trade secrets needs robust protection. Security is not an afterthought; it's a fundamental design principle. We must consider secure authentication and authorization mechanisms, protect against common web vulnerabilities such as SQL injection, XSS and CSRF, and stay compliant with data privacy regulations.
- **Maintainability:** These applications evolve over time as business needs change, and technologies improve. A well-structured, maintainable codebase saves time, reduces costs, and prevents headaches. Maintainability is also about code readability, modularity, and having good documentation practices, and consistent code styles.
- **Integration:** Enterprise applications rarely live in isolation. They must seamlessly integrate with other systems and services through APIs. This includes authentication, data exchanges, notifications and real time interactions. The ability to work with different systems ensures a holistic solution.
- **Performance:** For enterprise applications, performance is about responsiveness. Users need to complete their tasks smoothly, without delays. Slow loading times, lagging interactions, and poor performance can directly impact user productivity and customer experience. It's also crucial for SEO optimization if the application is customer facing.
- **Accessibility:** Ensuring accessibility for users with disabilities is not just ethical; it's often a legal requirement. An accessible application means that everyone, irrespective of their physical or cognitive ability, can navigate and use the application effectively. This requires careful design, using ARIA attributes and following accessibility guidelines.

A Personal Insight

From my experiences, the most common pitfall I've seen is neglecting maintainability and security early on. Developers often focus on quickly building the core functionalities, overlooking best practices for long-term success. It's like building a house without a proper foundation - problems become more difficult and expensive to solve later on.

Practical Considerations

It is also important to consider these:

- **User Experience (UX):** A poorly designed user experience will lead to user dissatisfaction. Usability testing and iterative design are very important.
- **Cost-effectiveness:** While building enterprise applications is costly, you must choose technologies and development processes that allow you to keep costs under control.
- **Team Collaboration:** Many developers work on enterprise applications, so it's important to have processes that ensure seamless collaboration.

In Summary

Building enterprise web applications requires a mindset shift. You're not just building features, but a reliable, secure, and scalable system that supports business objectives. To create successful enterprise web solutions, we must deeply understand the key characteristics that define them. By considering these characteristics, we can make better decisions as we move through the development process.

In the next sections, we will explore how Next.js 15 helps address these needs.

1.2 THE BENEFITS OF CHOOSING NEXT.JS 15

We've established what makes enterprise web applications unique. Now, let's talk about why Next.js 15 is an excellent choice for tackling those challenges. Choosing the right framework is crucial, it can make your project development enjoyable, and successful.

Next.js isn't just another JavaScript framework. It's a powerful tool designed to handle the complexities of modern web development, particularly for ambitious projects like enterprise applications. It offers a blend of performance, scalability, and a smooth developer experience, making it a popular choice for both startups and established organizations.

Performance: Speed and Efficiency

One of the standout features of Next.js is its focus on performance right out of the box. This is primarily achieved through:

- **Server-Side Rendering (SSR):** Unlike traditional client-side rendered apps where the browser does all the work, Next.js can render the initial HTML on the server. This makes initial load times significantly faster, improves SEO, and results in a better user experience. Think of it as delivering a complete meal rather than just the ingredients.
- **Static Site Generation (SSG):** For content that doesn't change often, Next.js can generate static HTML at build time. This means faster page loads, less server load, and higher scalability. It's like creating a pre-built website for the user.
- **Image Optimization:** Next.js comes with built-in image optimization, ensuring that images load quickly without compromising on quality. It automatically serves images in the optimal format and size, improving load times.
- **Code Splitting:** Next.js automatically splits your JavaScript bundle, so users only download the necessary code for a specific page. This technique further enhances page load speed and overall performance.

As someone who has worked on large web applications, I can vouch for the impact these optimizations make. The difference in user experience is substantial. When an application is fast and smooth, you notice it.

Scalability: Handling Growth and Complexity

Enterprise applications need to scale. Next.js offers robust mechanisms for this:

- **Incremental Static Regeneration (ISR):** With ISR, you can generate static pages that update periodically. This combines the benefits of both SSR and SSG. It's a good approach when your application has frequently updated data.

- **API Routes:** Next.js makes it incredibly simple to create backend API endpoints directly within your application. This can be beneficial when you need to handle complex business logic.
- **Hybrid Rendering Strategies:** Next.js allows you to mix SSR and SSG, choosing the right approach for each page or section of your application. This flexibility means you can optimize performance and scalability according to your needs.
- **Serverless Functions:** Next.js makes it easy to integrate serverless functions for computationally intensive tasks. Serverless is a great option for scalability and cost effectiveness.

Next.js allows us to scale our application based on our needs without a major refactor, which is crucial in an enterprise setting.

Developer Experience: Productivity and Efficiency

The developer experience is often overlooked, but it is important. Next.js excels in this area:

- **Fast Refresh:** When you make changes to your code, Next.js automatically updates your browser instantly. It feels like a seamless, non-stop process.
- **Intuitive Routing:** Creating pages and setting up routes is straightforward. The file-based routing makes navigation easy to manage.
- **Component-Based Architecture:** Next.js leverages React's component-based architecture, making your code modular, reusable, and easier to manage.
- **TypeScript Support:** Next.js has first class support for TypeScript. This can greatly reduce bugs and improve code maintainability, especially in large teams.

From my personal experience, a good developer experience makes a huge difference in productivity and overall happiness of the team. We do not have to worry so much about configuration and deployment. We focus on building great experiences.

Full-Stack Capabilities

Next.js isn't just for the frontend. With Next.js, you can also build your backend logic within the same project.

- **Server Actions**: Allows you to perform server side actions directly from your React components
- **API Routes:** Allows you to build API endpoints within your application.
- **Middleware:** You can implement middleware functions to handle authentication, redirection, and other tasks.
- **Database Integrations:** You can directly connect to various databases using libraries such as Prisma and Drizzle.

Next.js allows you to build your entire application in one place, simplifies your tech stack, and streamlines your development workflow.

Active Community and Ecosystem

Next.js has a thriving community and ecosystem:

- **Extensive Documentation:** The documentation is very detailed.
- **Rich Libraries and Tools:** You will find a rich amount of tools and libraries to improve your development process.
- **Strong Community Support:** You will find online communities where you can ask questions and get help.

The community and ecosystem can greatly improve your experience building with Next.js.

Practical Implementation

Let's create a basic API endpoint:

1. Inside your src/app directory create api/hello/route.js

```
import { NextResponse } from 'next/server';

export async function GET() {
  return NextResponse.json({ message: 'Hello from Next.js API' });
}
```

2. Open your browser and go to http://localhost:3000/api/hello, you should see the JSON response.

This example is basic, but it demonstrates how easy it is to create API endpoints with Next.js.

Final Thoughts

Next.js 15 brings a lot to the table, making it an excellent option for enterprise applications. It offers performance, scalability, a superb developer experience, and the ability to handle full-stack development. By choosing Next.js you are investing in the future of your project.

In the following sections we will start putting some of these concepts to practice. Is there anything specific you'd like to discuss further?

1.3 SETTING UP YOUR ENTERPRISE DEVELOPMENT ENVIRONMENT

A well-configured development environment is the cornerstone of successful enterprise projects. It's not just about having the right tools; it's about establishing a consistent, collaborative, and efficient workflow for your team. Think of this environment as your workshop – it needs to be organized, well-lit, and equipped with everything you need to build something great.

In this section, we'll cover the essentials: project structure, code style, version control, and environment management. We will be using VSCode, Git, Node.js and npm, but the principles can be applied to other tools too.

Project Structure: The Foundation for Maintainability

How you structure your project significantly impacts its long-term maintainability and scalability. A well-organized project is easier to navigate, debug, and extend.

The default Next.js project structure is a good starting point, with a src folder containing your app directory. However, for enterprise applications, we need to go a step further:

- **Feature-Based Organization:** Instead of organizing files by type (e.g., all components in one directory, all pages in another), we can group them by feature. For example, the login feature would contain all the components, logic, and tests related to logging in. This makes it easier to find relevant code.

```
    src/
app/
  auth/
    login/
      page.tsx
      components/
        LoginForm.tsx
      utils/
      tests/
```

- **Separation of Concerns:** Keep your business logic separate from your presentation logic. Place your data fetching code, utility functions, and other business logic in dedicated folders, making sure your React components are focused solely on the UI.
- **Clear Naming Conventions:** Use consistent and descriptive names for your files and folders, making it easy to understand what they contain.

A clear project structure, even though seems minor, can greatly improve the development experience, especially as your project grows.

Code Style and Tooling: Ensuring Consistency

In enterprise settings, multiple developers contribute to the project, therefore it is critical that everyone follows the same style rules. Inconsistency in code style leads to confusion and makes the codebase more difficult to work with.

- **Linters (ESLint):** ESLint helps you identify and fix coding errors, enforce coding styles, and prevent potential issues. You can customize ESLint to work for your needs by creating your own rules or using a ready-made configuration.
- **Formatters (Prettier):** Prettier automatically formats your code, ensuring consistency across your project. Prettier makes your code look tidy and readable.
- **Editor Configuration:** By integrating ESLint and Prettier with your code editor, you can enforce coding style as you code, and get

feedback immediately. VSCode supports both, making code editing more convenient.

To illustrate, let's see how to integrate these into our VSCode editor.

1. **Install ESLint and Prettier extensions** in VSCode.
2. **Configure ESLint:** In the .eslintrc.json file, add configurations as you see fit. Here is an example:

```
{
"extends": [
  "eslint:recommended",
  "plugin:@typescript-eslint/recommended",
  "next/core-web-vitals",
   "prettier"
],
"parser": "@typescript-eslint/parser",
"plugins": ["@typescript-eslint"],
"rules": {
  "no-console": "warn",
  "no-unused-vars": "warn",
  "react/no-unescaped-entities": "off"
}
}
```

Here you are adding some rules and extending the recommended configurations.

3. **Configure Prettier:** Add a .prettierrc.json file in your project root and customize the rules:

```
{
"semi": true,
"trailingComma": "all",
"singleQuote": true,
"printWidth": 100,
"tabWidth": 2
```

```
}
```

4. **Configure VSCode:** In settings.json in VSCode add:

```
"editor.formatOnSave": true,
"editor.defaultFormatter": "esbenp.prettier-vscode",
"editor.codeActionsOnSave": {
  "source.fixAll.eslint": true
},
```

By doing this, every time you save, your code will be formatted by Prettier and ESLint will be applied, fixing any issues.

Adopting these tools is not just about formatting, it makes you a better developer and your code more readable and maintainable.

TypeScript: Type Safety for Large Projects

TypeScript provides static typing, which helps catch errors during development, rather than in production. It enhances code quality, improves readability, and makes the codebase easier to maintain.

While we selected TypeScript during the setup, let's reinforce this with an example.

1. In src/app/auth/login/components/LoginForm.tsx:

```
interface LoginFormProps {
  onSubmit: (data: { username: string; password: string }) =>
void;
}

const LoginForm: React.FC<LoginFormProps> = ({ onSubmit }) =>
{
  const handleSubmit = (e: React.FormEvent) => {
    e.preventDefault();
    const username = (e.target as
HTMLFormElement).username.value;
```

```
    const password = (e.target as
HTMLFormElement).password.value;

    onSubmit({ username, password });
  };


  return (
    <form onSubmit={handleSubmit}>
        <input type="text" name="username"
placeholder="Username" />
        <input type="password" name="password"
placeholder="Password" />
        <button type="submit">Login</button>
    </form>
  );
};


export default LoginForm;
```

With this example, we have defined a data type for the form onSubmit function, which helps us catch errors early in the development process.

TypeScript may seem like it adds complexity, but it actually reduces bugs in the long run and enhances the robustness of enterprise code.

Git: Collaborative Version Control

Git is essential for collaborative development. It allows you to track changes, manage versions, and collaborate with your team.

For enterprise projects, you'll want to establish a clear branching strategy:

- **Main Branch:** Stable code in production.
- **Develop Branch:** Integrates all the latest features.
- **Feature Branches:** Develop each feature on a separate branch, which you then merge into develop after code reviews.

This ensures a stable process and allows developers to work collaboratively. The idea is to keep development organized and avoid conflicting changes.

Managing Environment Variables: Configuration Management

Enterprise applications often require different configurations for different environments (development, staging, production). We need to be very careful in managing sensitive information and environment variables such as API keys, database URLs, etc.

Next.js uses .env files to manage environment variables. To implement these:

1. Create three files at the root of your project: .env.local, .env.development, and .env.production.
2. In each file, set the environment variables:

```
.env.local:
NEXT_PUBLIC_API_URL = http://localhost:3000/api
```

```
.env.development:
NEXT_PUBLIC_API_URL = https://dev.example.com/api
```

```
.env.production:
NEXT_PUBLIC_API_URL = https://prod.example.com/api
```

.

In this example, we set a different API URL for each environment.

3. You can use these variables in the application:

```
const apiUrl = process.env.NEXT_PUBLIC_API_URL;
```

This is a straightforward way to handle different configurations without hardcoding them into your code.

My Personal Experience

I have personally seen that setting up the development environment upfront greatly improves team productivity and reduces frustration. It also helps onboard new developers as they can pick up the project easier.

Wrapping Up

A well-configured development environment is a gift to yourself. By carefully selecting your tools and processes, you'll set yourself for a much more efficient development.

In the next section, we will explore the challenges and considerations for developing large scale application.

1.4 CHALLENGES AND CONSIDERATIONS FOR LARGE-SCALE APPS

So, you've got your environment set up, you're familiar with Next.js 15's benefits, and you're ready to build something impressive. But let's pause for a moment and talk about the realities of building large-scale web applications. It's not just about adding more features; it's also about dealing with increased complexity, maintaining performance, and ensuring stability as your project grows.

Complexity: Taming the Beast

As your application grows, so does its complexity. This complexity can manifest in various ways:

- **Feature Bloat:** The application grows and features multiply, making it difficult to manage and maintain.
- **Interdependencies:** Components become tightly coupled, making it hard to modify or test them independently.
- **Code Sprawl:** The codebase becomes large and disorganized, making it difficult to navigate and understand.

To address these issues, it's crucial to adopt strategies that promote modularity, separation of concerns, and clear architectural patterns. This is about thinking long-term from day one. As developers, we should never stop thinking about the long-term maintainability and scalability of the code we are creating.

Team Collaboration: The Art of Working Together

Large projects mean larger teams, and collaboration becomes key. Some of the challenges you need to consider are:

- **Code Conflicts:** When multiple developers work on the same codebase, conflicts are inevitable. Clear communication, well-defined branching strategies, and consistent code styles can help.
- **Knowledge Sharing:** It's very important to share knowledge to avoid single points of failure.
- **Onboarding:** Onboarding new developers can be challenging if the project lacks proper documentation.
- **Consistency:** Maintaining consistency in code style, architecture, and processes across the team is key.

To mitigate these challenges:

- **Code Reviews:** Implementing code reviews helps catch bugs, share knowledge, and ensure code quality.
- **Documentation:** Well-maintained documentation makes it easier for team members to understand the codebase and how different components work.
- **Team Communication:** Daily stand-up meetings and team chats help keep everyone aligned.
- **Mentorship:** Pairing experienced developers with new team members helps share best practices and onboard new colleagues.

From my experience, an effective development process can greatly enhance collaboration, productivity, and the overall quality of the application. A well-functioning team can achieve a lot more than a disorganized one.

Performance at Scale: Keeping Things Speedy

As user base grows, performance issues can arise if not handled properly:

- **Slow Loading Times:** As more features are added, the initial page load time might increase.
- **Database Bottlenecks:** The database can become slow, particularly when processing large amounts of data.
- **API Performance:** API calls can become slow when there are multiple users and data to process.

To solve these issues:

- **Code Optimization:** Apply techniques like code splitting, lazy loading, and image optimization.
- **Database Optimization:** Ensure proper database indexing, query optimization and caching mechanisms.
- **Caching:** Implement caching strategies both on the client and server side to reduce load times.
- **Monitoring:** Use monitoring tools to identify performance bottlenecks in the system.

Performance is not a one-time activity, it's something you must constantly monitor, improve, and tweak as your application grows.

Security: Protecting Your Assets

As an application grows in scale and complexity, security becomes even more critical. You should be considering:

- **Vulnerabilities:** Large projects may have more security vulnerabilities due to complex dependencies and interactions.
- **Data Breaches:** Protecting sensitive data is critical. A data breach can have catastrophic consequences.
- **API Security:** APIs need to be secured to prevent unauthorized access.

Implementing security best practices is essential:

- **Input Sanitization:** Carefully sanitize inputs to avoid vulnerabilities such as SQL injection and cross-site scripting.
- **Authentication and Authorization:** Robust authentication and authorization mechanisms should be in place to ensure that only authorized users access the application.
- **Regular Audits:** Security audits and penetration testing can reveal potential vulnerabilities that are not apparent during the development process.

Security should be an integral part of the development process, not an afterthought. As developers, we should always prioritize security in all development decisions we make.

Long-Term Maintenance: Planning for the Future

It is very common that an application evolves over the time. You need to be prepared for the changes and the maintenance the application may require.

- **Code Refactoring:** As the application evolves, code refactoring will be necessary to improve code quality and performance.
- **Tech Debt:** Over time, the technical debt of the application might increase as new features are implemented.
- **Evolving Technologies:** New technologies and best practices can emerge, and the application might need to adapt.

To handle long-term maintenance:

- **Regular Code Reviews:** Continuous code reviews are a must to make sure the code is maintainable.
- **Documentation:** Maintain documentation up-to-date to help new developers understand the system.
- **Refactoring:** Dedicate time to refactor and update the code.
- **Adopting new tech:** Evaluate new technologies and best practices and adopt those as you see fit.

Planning for the long-term is a continuous process. It helps in keeping your application healthy over time.

Practical Example

Let's look at a simple example that can help with performance. When fetching a list of users, avoid loading all the users if you do not need them. Implement pagination instead:

```
const fetchUsers = async (page: number, limit: number) => {
  const res = await fetch(`/api/users?page=${page}&limit=${limit}`);
  const users = await res.json();
  return users;
};

const UsersList = () => {
  const [users, setUsers] = useState([]);
  const [page, setPage] = useState(1);
  const limit = 10;
```

```
useEffect(() => {
  fetchUsers(page, limit).then(setUsers);
}, [page]);

const handleNext = () => setPage((prev) => prev + 1);
const handlePrevious = () => setPage((prev) =>
Math.max(prev - 1, 1));
};
```

With this approach, we avoid loading all the users at once. We only load the users we need, improving the initial load time of the application.

Wrapping Up

Building large-scale applications is not easy, but by understanding the challenges and considering these issues as you design your system, you will build high quality and resilient enterprise applications.

In the next chapter we will start exploring more of the code that will help us build great enterprise applications with Next.js. Are you ready to move on?

CHAPTER 2: CORE NEXT.JS 15 CONCEPTS FOR ENTERPRISE

With a good grasp of the challenges involved in building large applications, we now turn our attention to the core concepts that Next.js 15 offers. These features are the tools you'll use to build high-performing and maintainable systems. Let's break them down one by one, focusing on their strategic application in an enterprise setting.

2.1 APP ROUTER VS. PAGES ROUTER: STRATEGIC APPLICATION

The introduction of the App Router in Next.js 13 was a significant shift, presenting developers with a choice: stick with the familiar Pages Router or embrace the new approach. This decision isn't just about personal preference; it's about strategically selecting the right tool for your project's current and future needs. Let's unravel these two routing approaches, emphasizing their differences, strengths, and when you should strategically choose one over the other.

Understanding the Pages Router (the Classic Approach)

The Pages Router, located in the pages/ directory, is how Next.js handled routing from the beginning. It's straightforward: each file in pages/ becomes a route, and the file structure mirrors the URL structure. For example, a file named pages/about.js or pages/about/index.js would be accessible via the /about route.

This simplicity is the Pages Router's greatest strength. It's easy to grasp, quick to set up, and works well for small to medium-sized applications. It also supports server-side rendering and static site generation out of the box.

However, the Pages Router has limitations, especially when building complex enterprise applications:

- **Limited Layout Options:** Sharing layouts across different pages can become cumbersome, making the code less maintainable.

- **No Server Components:** You are not able to take advantage of the server component benefits and all code runs in the client.
- **Data Fetching in components** Data fetching is usually done in the page component. The logic and structure becomes complex when there are many components and data fetching is needed on each component.
- **Scalability:** As the application grows, managing routes in the pages/ directory can become a little messy.

The App Router: Embracing the Future

The App Router, housed in the app/ directory, is a significant upgrade that addresses many of the Pages Router's limitations. It offers a more flexible and powerful way to manage routing and application structure. Key features include:

- **Layouts:** Layouts in the app/ directory are much easier to manage. You can have global layouts, nested layouts, etc. They help you build consistent experiences across all pages.
- **Server Components:** The App Router fully embraces server components, optimizing performance by rendering code on the server.
- **Nested Routes:** Creating nested routes is simple, making your application very modular.
- **Data Fetching:** You can perform data fetching directly within components using server components, which enhances readability and organization.
- **Colocation:** The App Router helps you organize components alongside your page code. For example, app/blog/[slug]/page.tsx can have all the related components inside the same slug directory.

The App Router takes some getting used to, but the advantages are considerable. It helps you build larger, more complex applications with greater efficiency and performance.

Strategic Application: When to Use Which

The most important part is knowing when to choose one router over the other.

- **New Projects: App Router is the recommended approach** for all new projects. It has better performance characteristics, a better developer experience, and it aligns with the future of Next.js. Choosing the App Router will ensure that your application is ready for future technologies and upgrades.

- **Existing Projects:** Migrating from the Pages Router to the App Router is not always a simple task. It might require changes to your existing code. You can consider this:
    - o **Incremental Migration:** Start using the App Router for new features and gradually migrate the old routes from pages/ over time.
    - o **Keep Legacy Routes:** If the migration to the App Router is too complex for your project, you might want to keep some legacy routes and implement the App Router in newer sections of the application.
    - o **Assess the Benefits:** Evaluate the need to move to the App Router for your existing projects. If the benefits are considerable (e.g., server components, layouts) it makes sense to start the migration process.
- **Hybrid Approach:** It is possible to use both App Router and Pages Router in your project. You can have a pages/ directory and an app/ directory at the same time. This allows you to migrate gradually and choose the appropriate routing system for different parts of your application.

Practical Example: Pages Router

In the pages/ directory, let's create about.js:

```
function AboutPage() {
return (
  <div>
    <h1>About Us</h1>
    <p>This is our about page</p>
  </div>
);
}

export default AboutPage;
```

This code will be available on the /about path. This approach is simple and great for simple pages. However, it is limited for complex applications.

Practical Example: App Router

In the app/ directory, let's create about/page.tsx:

```
export default function AboutPage() {
return (
  <div>
    <h1>About Us</h1>
    <p>This is our about page</p>
  </div>
);
}
```

This page will also be available on the /about path. We get the same functionality, but under the new App Router structure, which allows us to have more power. The App Router allows for server components, layouts, more flexible data fetching, and nested routing.

My Experience

From personal experience, when I first moved to the App Router, it felt a little daunting due to the new paradigm. However, once I got used to the new structure, I realized that it was much more flexible, and scalable. By planning the migration well, and doing it gradually, it helps to minimize disruption.

In Summary

Choosing between the App Router and the Pages Router is not just about preference, but it's about making a strategic choice that fits your project's current and future needs. By choosing the right approach for each scenario, you'll be able to create scalable, and maintainable enterprise applications.

In the next section, we will discuss Server and Client components, which are fundamental for using the App Router. Any questions before moving on?

2.2 SERVER AND CLIENT COMPONENTS: USAGE & TRADE-OFFS

With the introduction of the App Router in Next.js 13, we've moved into an era of component architecture that requires a shift in mindset: the distinction between Server Components and Client Components. Understanding how these components work, their capabilities, and when to use each is essential for building high-performance, scalable applications. Let's explore these concepts and analyze the trade-offs involved.

Server Components: Rendering on the Server

Server Components, by default, are the fundamental components in the app/ directory. They execute solely on the server, generating HTML that is then sent to the browser. This capability opens a world of possibilities for performance optimization and data handling. Server components:

- **Fetch Data Directly:** They can fetch data directly from databases, APIs, or the file system. This is fantastic because you can execute data fetching logic on the server, and avoid exposing database keys and secrets.
- **Render on the Server:** This improves initial load times. It also helps SEO, as search engines can easily parse content rendered on the server.
- **No Browser APIs:** Server Components do not have access to browser APIs (e.g. window, localStorage). This limitation ensures that these components focus solely on server-side operations.
- **No client interactivity:** You cannot use features that depend on browser interactivity such as hooks (useState, useEffect).
- **Improved Security:** Server components can keep API keys, secrets and business logic out of the client-side code, improving overall security.

Server Components are a game changer, moving computationally intensive tasks to the server, improving performance, and helping to create applications that are more efficient and secure.

Client Components: Interactivity in the Browser

Client Components, marked by the "use client" directive, run within the user's browser. They are essential for building interactive user interfaces:

- **Access to Browser APIs:** Client Components have access to browser APIs, enabling user interactions and state management.
- **State Management:** You can use React hooks like useState, useEffect, and useContext to manage state.
- **Event Handling:** They can handle user events such as clicks, form submissions, mouse movements, etc.
- **Client-Side Interactivity:** They render and update dynamically in the browser.

Client components are the go to when you need to add a UI that has interactions with the user.

Usage and Trade-offs: Finding the Balance

The key to leveraging Server and Client components is understanding their strengths, limitations, and how to combine them effectively:

- **Server Components for Data Fetching and Rendering:** Use Server Components for tasks like fetching data, rendering content, and handling server-side logic. This makes your application faster for the initial load.
- **Client Components for Interactivity and State Management:** Use Client Components when you need to add interactive features, manage user interfaces, and handle client-side state.
- **Minimize Client Component Usage:** If a component does not need browser interactivity, you should make it a server component. This helps to reduce the overall bundle size and improve load times.
- **Create Reusable Components:** Create reusable components that can be used in different parts of your application. It helps you to keep your code DRY (Don't Repeat Yourself), and improves maintainability.

Practical Implementation

Let's see a practical example. First, let's create a Server Component in src/app/components/ServerComponent.tsx:

```
// This is a server component
interface Props {
```

```
    message: string;
}


const ServerComponent: React.FC<Props> = async ({ message })
=> {
  const data = await fetchMyData()
  return (
    <div>
      <h1>{message}</h1>
        {data.map(item => <p key={item.id}>{item.name}</p>)}
    </div>
  );
};


async function fetchMyData() {
   const res = await
fetch('https://jsonplaceholder.typicode.com/users')
   return res.json()
}
export default ServerComponent;
```

**Now, let's create a Client Component
src/app/components/ClientComponent.tsx:**

```
      'use client';
import React, { useState } from 'react';


interface Props {
  initialCount: number;
}


const ClientComponent: React.FC<Props> = ({ initialCount })
=> {
  const [count, setCount] = useState(initialCount);


  return (
```

```
    <div>
      <p>Count: {count}</p>
      <button onClick={() => setCount(count +
1)}>Increment</button>
    </div>
  );
};


export default ClientComponent;
```

Now in src/app/page.tsx let's use these components:

```
      import ClientComponent from
'./components/ClientComponent'
import ServerComponent from './components/ServerComponent'

export default function Home() {
  return (
    <main>
      <ServerComponent message="Hello from Server Component"
/>
      <ClientComponent initialCount={0} />
    </main>
  );
}
```

In this example, the ServerComponent fetches data from an API and renders it on the server. The ClientComponent has an interactive button which increments the counter. By combining them, we have a server rendered page with interactive components.

My Personal Experience

Initially, the distinction between Server and Client Components can feel a bit complex, but when understood, it opens doors to incredible optimizations. It helps you to approach problems from a different perspective. I found that it makes it very easy to organize my application based on interactivity and data fetching requirements, which leads to a cleaner codebase.

In Summary

Understanding and strategically applying Server and Client components is essential for building scalable and performant enterprise applications. By effectively combining these components, you can enhance the user experience, improve performance, and create applications that are more secure and maintainable.

In the next section, we will discuss data fetching and how to optimize your application for performance and SEO.

2.3 DATA FETCHING: OPTIMIZING FOR PERFORMANCE AND SEO

In the realm of web development, data fetching is a crucial aspect that directly impacts both the user experience and search engine optimization (SEO). Next.js 15 provides powerful and flexible ways to fetch data, but it also requires a strategic approach to ensure optimal performance and SEO. Let's dive into how to master data fetching in Next.js and understand its nuances.

Understanding the Core Concepts

At the heart of data fetching lies the question: Where and when should your data be retrieved? Next.js offers three primary approaches:

1. **Server-Side Rendering (SSR):** Data is fetched on the server during each request. This results in a fully rendered HTML page, which is sent to the client. It's great for dynamic content and SEO, but it can be slower due to the extra server processing for every request.
2. **Static Site Generation (SSG):** Data is fetched at build time, generating static HTML pages. This results in blazingly fast loading times, but it is ideal for content that does not change very often, such as a blog or a documentation site.
3. **Client-Side Data Fetching:** Data is fetched in the browser after the initial HTML load. This can be suitable for interactive, user-specific

components, but it does not help with SEO or initial load performance.

Server-Side Rendering (SSR): Fetching on Demand

With SSR, the server fetches the required data, generates HTML, and sends the result to the client. This ensures that the user gets a fully rendered page, ideal for SEO, as search engines can parse the content easily.

- **When to use:** Use SSR for pages that require dynamic content, personalized data, or when SEO is critical.
- **How it Works:** You fetch data in your Server Components, which runs on the server.
- **Trade-offs:** SSR is great for SEO and dynamic content, but can be slower because of server processing overhead for each request.

Practical Example:

In src/app/products/page.tsx:

```
async function fetchProducts() {
  const res = await
fetch('https://fakestoreapi.com/products');
  return res.json();
}


export default async function ProductsPage() {
  const products = await fetchProducts();
  return (
    <div>
      <h1>Product List</h1>
        {products.map(product => <p
key={product.id}>{product.title}</p>)}
    </div>
  );
}
```

Here, we use SSR to fetch and render a list of products.

Static Site Generation (SSG): Pre-Rendering at Build Time

SSG generates static HTML at build time. These pages are then served directly from a CDN without any server-side processing.

- **When to use:** Use SSG for content that doesn't change often, such as documentation pages, blogs, or marketing pages.
- **How it works:** Next.js generates the HTML during the build process.
- **Trade-offs:** SSG is great for performance and SEO, but not recommended for frequently changing data, as the data is static.

Practical Example:

In src/app/blog/page.tsx:

```
async function fetchBlogPosts() {
  const res = await
fetch('https://jsonplaceholder.typicode.com/posts');
  return res.json();
}


export default async function BlogPage() {
  const posts = await fetchBlogPosts();
  return (
    <div>
      <h1>Blog Posts</h1>
      {posts.map((post) => <p
key={post.id}>{post.title}</p>)}
    </div>
  );
}
```

This example generates the blog posts at build time.

Client-Side Data Fetching: When Interactivity is Key

Client-side data fetching happens in the browser, often used for components that need to manage state and handle user interaction.

- **When to use:** Use Client-side data fetching for specific UI features, or when you need real-time user-specific data.
- **How it works:** Fetch data in your Client Components by using hooks like useEffect.
- **Trade-offs:** It is less effective for SEO, and the data may not be immediately visible, increasing time to interactivity.

Practical Example:

In src/app/components/ClientDataComponent.tsx:

```tsx
'use client';
import { useState, useEffect } from 'react';

interface User {
  id: number;
  name: string;
}

const ClientDataComponent = () => {
  const [users, setUsers] = useState<User[]>([]);

  useEffect(() => {
    fetch('https://jsonplaceholder.typicode.com/users')
      .then((res) => res.json())
      .then(setUsers);
  }, []);

  return (
    <div>
      <h1>Client Side Users</h1>
        {users.map((user) => (
          <p key={user.id}>{user.name}</p>
        ))}
    </div>
```

```
  );
};
export default ClientDataComponent;
```

In this example, the user list is fetched client side using useEffect.

Incremental Static Regeneration (ISR): The Best of Both Worlds

ISR allows you to generate static pages that update periodically. This combines the best of both SSG and SSR.

- **When to use:** Use ISR for data that changes occasionally, for example dashboards, or product pages.
- **How it works:** You configure the time to refresh the static data.
- **Trade-offs:** ISR gives you static performance while allowing dynamic updates.

Practical Example

In src/app/dashboard/page.tsx you can add revalidate

```
    export const revalidate = 60; //revalidate every 60
seconds.

async function fetchDashboardData() {
  const res = await fetch('https://example.com/dashboard', {
    next: { revalidate: 60 },
  });
  return res.json();
}
export default async function DashboardPage(){
    const data = await fetchDashboardData();

    return(
      <div>
         <h1>Dashboard</h1>
           <p>Latest data: {data.date}</p>
      </div>
```

```
    )

}
```

In this example, the dashboard page is regenerated every 60 seconds.

Optimizing for Performance and SEO

- **Cache Data:** Implement caching mechanisms both on the client and the server side. This helps to reduce loading times.
- **Optimize Data Transfer:** Implement techniques to compress your data, optimizing bandwidth usage.
- **Prefetch data:** Use prefetching to load resources before they are needed.
- **Server-Side Fetching:** Prefer server-side data fetching whenever possible, to improve SEO and initial load times.
- **SEO in Mind:** Always consider SEO when making your data fetching decisions. Make sure that important information is server rendered.

Personal Insight

I've learned from experience that choosing the right data fetching strategy can dramatically impact your application's performance and SEO. Understanding the differences between each technique, and adopting them strategically, is critical for a successful enterprise application. I recommend that you adopt a pragmatic approach, and consider each strategy for each scenario you find yourself.

Summary

Data fetching is a core aspect of Next.js 15, offering great flexibility and power. You can build blazing fast applications that have great SEO by combining SSR, SSG, Client Side fetching, and ISR strategically.

In the next section, we will discuss Layouts, Metadata, and Templates and how they can improve your application's design consistency and branding.

2.4 LAYOUTS, METADATA, AND TEMPLATING: BRANDING AT SCALE

When building an enterprise application, consistency and branding are paramount. It's not just about the functionality; it's also about creating a cohesive experience that reinforces your brand identity. Next.js 15 provides powerful mechanisms for achieving this through layouts, metadata, and templating. Let's explore how these tools can help you maintain a consistent look and feel across your application.

Layouts: Establishing Consistency

Layouts are components that wrap around your pages, providing a shared structure for your application. They can contain headers, footers, sidebars, or any other element that you want to share across multiple pages.

- **How They Work:** Layouts are created within the app directory. The layout.tsx file acts as the root layout for the directory. You can create nested layouts by creating layout.tsx files in subdirectories.
- **Benefits:** Layouts improve consistency, eliminate redundant code, and simplify the development process by allowing you to create shared UI patterns.
- **Server Components:** Layouts are server components by default, so you can use server side data fetching to fetch data for your layouts.

Practical Implementation:

In src/app/layout.tsx:

```
import './globals.css';
import Header from './components/Header';
import Footer from './components/Footer';

export const metadata = {
  title: 'My Enterprise Application',
  description: 'An enterprise application built with Next.js 15',
};


export default function RootLayout({
  children,
}: {
```

```
  children: React.ReactNode;
}) {
  return (
    <html lang="en">
      <body>
        <Header/>
        {children}
       <Footer />
      </body>
    </html>
  );
}
```

In this example, the RootLayout is a root layout for all pages within your app directory, that renders a Header and Footer on every page. This code helps establish a consistent look and feel across all the pages in the application.

You can also create nested layouts. In src/app/dashboard/layout.tsx:

```
import Sidebar from './components/Sidebar';

export default function DashboardLayout({
  children,
}: {
  children: React.ReactNode;
}) {
  return (
    <div style={{ display: 'flex' }}>
        <Sidebar/>
      <main style={{ flex: 1, padding: '20px'
}}>{children}</main>
    </div>
  );
}
```

In this example, the DashboardLayout wraps all pages under the dashboard/ directory, adding a Sidebar.

Layouts make it easier to manage shared components and ensure a consistent layout across different parts of the application.

Metadata: Essential for SEO and Branding

Metadata, like titles and descriptions, is essential for SEO, branding, and sharing.

- **How it Works:** In Next.js, you define metadata using the metadata object, which is exported from layout.tsx or page.tsx files.
- **Benefits:** Well-defined metadata helps search engines to understand your content, improves your search ranking, and makes your pages more shareable.

Practical Implementation:

In the root layout, you have this metadata in src/app/layout.tsx:

```
export const metadata = {
  title: 'My Enterprise Application',
  description: 'An enterprise application built with Next.js
15',
};
```

You can customize your metadata for each page:

In src/app/blog/[slug]/page.tsx:

```
export const metadata = {
  title: 'My blog post title',
  description: 'My blog post description',
};
```

Metadata helps in improving your page's search engine visibility and ensuring consistency with your brand.

Templating: Reusable Design Elements

Templating allows you to create reusable design elements that can be used across your application. By creating reusable components, you are able to:

- **Maintain Consistency:** Avoid inconsistent designs, and maintain the same visual language across your application.
- **Save Time:** Create templates, rather than repeatedly building similar components.
- **Improve maintainability:** When you need to change a design, you change it in one place, and it is reflected everywhere.

Practical Implementation:

Let's create a button component in src/app/components/Button.tsx:

```
interface ButtonProps {
children: React.ReactNode;
onClick?: () => void;
type?: 'button' | 'submit' | 'reset';
className?: string
}


const Button: React.FC<ButtonProps> = ({ children, onClick,
type = 'button', className = '' }) => {
    return (
    <button className={`bg-blue-500 hover:bg-blue-700 text-
white py-2 px-4 rounded ${className}`}
            onClick={onClick} type={type}>
      {children}
    </button>
  );
};
export default Button;
```

In this example, we have created a reusable button with some default styling that we can use across our application.

Now you can use this button in your page:

```
    import Button from "../components/Button";

export default function AboutPage() {
  return (
    <div>
      <h1>About Us</h1>
      <p>This is our about page</p>
        <Button>Click Me</Button>
    </div>
  );
}
```

This shows that a simple button component can improve consistency and developer experience. You can implement other reusable components as your application needs.

My Experience

From my experiences building enterprise applications, I've seen the crucial impact that consistent design has on user engagement and brand perception. Using layouts, metadata, and templates not only makes the development process faster but also ensures a cohesive user experience across the whole application. This approach makes the code more scalable and helps your brand.

Summary

Next.js 15 provides great tools to establish consistency and branding at scale with layouts, metadata, and templates. By carefully implementing these, you can build an application that is visually and functionally cohesive, and also optimizes your brand.

In the next section, we will explore Advanced Routing and Navigation Patterns.

.

2.5 ADVANCED ROUTING AND NAVIGATION PATTERNS

Routing and navigation are fundamental to any web application, but as projects grow, so does the complexity of handling navigation efficiently. Next.js 15 offers a powerful system for handling complex routing and navigation patterns that are essential for enterprise applications. Let's explore some of these advanced techniques, and when to implement them.

Nested Routes: Organizing Your Application

Nested routes are routes that have a hierarchical structure. This pattern helps you to better organize your application, and create more complex layouts.

- **How they work:** You create nested routes by nesting directories inside your app/ directory.
- **Benefits:** Better organization of application code and routes, and the ability to create complex layouts and UIs.
- **Practical Use:** Imagine an e-commerce platform where you have /products/ for all products, and then /products/[id]/ for the specific product. This would be a perfect example of nested routes.

Practical Implementation:

Let's create a few nested routes.

1. Create a folder src/app/products/, and then create src/app/products/page.tsx:

```
export default function ProductsPage(){
return (
    <div>
        <h1>Products</h1>
        <p>This is the product list page</p>
    </div>
 )
}
```

2. Now, let's create a dynamic route. Create src/app/products/[id]/page.tsx:

```
export default function ProductDetails({params}:
{params: {id: string}}){
    return (
        <div>
          <h1>Product Detail</h1>
            <p>This is the product detail page
{params.id}</p>
        </div>
    )
}
```

In the example above, we have a nested route with a dynamic segment. The ProductDetails will be rendered when a request is made to /products/123 (where 123 is the dynamic segment), and the ProductsPage will be rendered when a request is made to /products.

Nested routes help to structure your application and keep it organized.

Dynamic Routes: Handling Data-Driven Pages

Dynamic routes allow you to handle pages where the URL segments vary based on the data.

- **How they work:** You define dynamic segments using square brackets (e.g., [id], [slug]).
- **Benefits:** Handles data-driven pages, makes it easy to build dynamic web applications, and simplifies routing for single-item resources.
- **Practical Use:** You use this approach every time you need to load resources based on the URL such as a blog post based on a slug, or a product based on an ID.

Practical Implementation:

We already saw this in the previous example with /products/[id]/page.tsx. The [id] will be dynamically filled using the URL.

Let's see another example in src/app/blog/[slug]/page.tsx :

46

```
    export default function BlogPost({params}: {params:
{slug: string}}){
    return (
      <div>
         <h1>Blog Post</h1>
            <p>This is the blog post page {params.slug}</p>
      </div>
    )
}
```

In this example the dynamic segment is slug, so a request to /blog/my-first-post will render the BlogPost component and the dynamic segment will be my-first-post.

Dynamic routes provide great flexibility when building data-driven applications.

Programmatic Navigation: Redirects and Page Transitions

Next.js provides the useRouter hook to navigate programmatically within your application.

- **How it works:** By using useRouter you have access to methods such as push, replace and back.
- **Benefits:** Makes it easy to redirect users, handle form submissions, and create custom navigation flows.
- **Practical Use:** When you submit a form, and you want to redirect to a different page. Or when you want to perform a redirect based on a condition, or when you want to go to the previous page.

Practical Implementation:

In src/app/components/NavigationButton.tsx

```
    'use client';
import { useRouter } from 'next/navigation'

interface NavigationButtonProps {
    path: string,
```

```
    text: string
}


const NavigationButton: React.FC<NavigationButtonProps> =
({path, text}) => {
  const router = useRouter();
  return (
    <button onClick={() => router.push(path)}>{text}</button>
  )
}
export default NavigationButton
```

Here we have created a reusable button that uses useRouter to redirect to a specific path.

Now let's use this component in a page:

```
import NavigationButton from "./components/NavigationButton";

export default function AboutPage() {
  return (
    <div>
      <h1>About Us</h1>
      <p>This is our about page</p>
        <NavigationButton path="/" text="Go to home"/>
    </div>
  );
}
```

Now, when the user clicks the Go to home button, it will redirect to the home page. This example shows that useRouter is a great way to manage programmatic navigation.

Route Handlers: API Endpoints Within Your App

Next.js allows you to create API endpoints within the same app/ directory. This is a great way to colocate your API endpoints alongside your UI.

- **How they work:** Create an api/ directory inside your app/ directory. A file inside the api/ directory becomes an API endpoint that can handle HTTP requests.
- **Benefits:** API endpoints are colocated with the UI, simplifying your project.
- **Practical Use:** Ideal for small backend services that require the same architecture as your user interface.

Practical Implementation:

Create src/app/api/hello/route.ts:

```
import { NextResponse } from 'next/server'

export async function GET() {
  return NextResponse.json({ message: 'Hello from my API' })
}
```

Now, you can make a request to http://localhost:3000/api/hello and you should receive the JSON response.

Route handlers make it easy to create API endpoints within the same project, reducing complexity and centralizing all code.

My Experience

From my experience, mastering these techniques is critical when building large applications. The power of nested routing, dynamic routes, and the navigation hooks, makes it easy to create a scalable and maintainable application. I suggest that you adopt a pragmatic approach, considering each technique based on your requirements.

Summary

Next.js 15 provides powerful routing and navigation techniques that allow you to build complex, dynamic applications. By combining these techniques, you can create a seamless experience for your users, while keeping your application organized and easy to maintain.

In the next chapter, we'll move on to architecting enterprise applications.

CHAPTER 3: BUILDING AN ENTERPRISE-READY WORKFLOW

Alright, we've covered the core Next.js 15 concepts and how to use them effectively. Now, let's shift gears and talk about the practical aspects of building enterprise-level applications. It's not just about the code; it's also about the processes and tools that help us write better code, collaborate more effectively, and deploy our applications reliably. In this chapter, we'll explore the foundational elements of an enterprise-ready workflow.

3.1 PROJECT STRUCTURE FOR MAINTAINABILITY

A well-defined project structure is the backbone of any scalable and maintainable application, especially in the enterprise landscape. Imagine building a house: you wouldn't just throw bricks together randomly, would you? You'd have a blueprint, a plan that outlines where everything goes. The same principle applies to code. A thoughtful project structure isn't just about aesthetics; it's about making your code easier to navigate, understand, and evolve over time.

In this section, we'll explore why project structure matters, the problems a poor structure can create, and how to implement a structure that sets you up for long-term success. Think of this as creating a well-organized library, where everything is easy to find and accessible.

Why Does Project Structure Matter?

In the early stages of a project, the organization of code might not seem crucial. However, as the application grows, the lack of a well-defined project structure can lead to a host of problems:

- **Difficulty Navigating the Codebase:** When files are scattered haphazardly, developers spend valuable time hunting for specific code, components, or functions, reducing productivity.
- **Increased Bug Potential:** Poorly structured code can increase the likelihood of errors as it becomes difficult to trace dependencies and logic flows.

- **Reduced Maintainability:** Code that is hard to navigate is also difficult to maintain. This increases technical debt, makes it hard to add features, and increases the risk of introducing bugs.
- **Collaboration Issues:** A poorly structured codebase makes it harder for team members to collaborate effectively. It can lead to conflicting changes, confusion, and duplicated effort.
- **Scalability Issues:** Applications with a disorganized structure struggle when they need to scale or when new team members are added to the team.

A well-defined structure helps prevent these issues, making the development process much more manageable. It's an investment that pays off in the long run.

The Feature-Based Structure: A Strategic Approach

Traditional project structures often group files by type, for example, all components in a components directory, and all pages in a pages directory. However, in large projects, a feature-based structure is usually a more effective approach.

In a feature-based structure, you group files by feature, or functionality rather than file type. For example, the auth feature would include everything related to authentication, such as the login page, register page, logout page, related components, utilities, and tests.

Benefits of Feature-Based Structure:

- **Improved Organization:** Features are grouped in one single place, improving developer experience and code readability.
- **Reduced Complexity:** Keeps the application focused on features instead of file types, making the project easier to navigate.
- **Enhanced Maintainability:** When you need to change or add something, all related files are in the same place, making the changes easier.
- **Better Collaboration:** When each team member works on a feature, they know where to find the related code.
- **Scalability:** Features are modular. You can add new features without disrupting existing code.

Practical Implementation:

Let's illustrate a feature-based project structure:

```
    src/
app/
  auth/
    login/
      page.tsx
      components/
        LoginForm.tsx
      utils/
      tests/
    register/
    logout/
  dashboard/
    page.tsx
    components/
      DashboardSummary.tsx
    utils/
  products/
    page.tsx
    [id]/
      page.tsx
  components/
      Button.tsx
      Card.tsx
  utils/
    api.ts
    helpers.ts
```

.

In this structure:

- The auth folder contains all features related to authentication (login, registration, logout)
- The dashboard folder contains all features related to the dashboard.
- The products folder contains everything related to products.

- The components folder contains reusable components such as Button or Card.
- The utils folder contains utility and helper functions such as API calls, date formatting, etc.

Key Principles for a Maintainable Project Structure:

- **Consistency:** Apply the same structure across all of your features and sections of the application.
- **Clarity:** Use clear, descriptive names for your folders and files.
- **Separation of Concerns:** Group related code together (e.g., business logic and UI, data access and presentation) to prevent code from becoming a tangled mess.
- **Modularity:** Break down complex features into smaller, more manageable modules. This will improve code reusability and testability.
- **Avoid Deep Nesting:** Keep your folder structure reasonably shallow to prevent overly complex file paths.
- **Keep it Flexible:** Your project structure should be flexible and allow your application to grow.

A Personal Insight

In my experience, spending time defining a well-structured project at the beginning of the project, will save a lot of time and frustration in the long run. I remember working on projects where the structure was not well planned, and it was incredibly difficult to make changes or add new features. It was painful. Taking the time to implement a structure saves your team from headaches down the road.

Practical Example: Separating Concerns

Let's create an example. In src/app/auth/login/page.tsx:

```
import LoginForm from './components/LoginForm';
import { loginUser } from './utils';


const LoginPage = () => {
  const handleSubmit = async (data: {username: string,
password: string}) => {
    await loginUser(data);
```

```
    };

    return (
      <div>
        <h1>Login</h1>
          <LoginForm onSubmit={handleSubmit} />
      </div>
    );
};

export default LoginPage;
```

In src/app/auth/login/utils.ts:

```
    export async function loginUser(data: {username:
string, password: string}) {
  const res = await fetch('/api/login', {
      method: 'POST',
    body: JSON.stringify(data),
  });
  return res.json();
}
```

In this example, the page file contains the presentation logic, and all the other code is in utils, keeping things separated.

In Summary

A well-thought-out project structure is a crucial component of any enterprise-ready application. By adopting a feature-based structure, clear naming conventions, and separating concerns, you'll make your code more maintainable, scalable, and enjoyable to work with.

In the next section, we will discuss the importance of consistent coding styles and how to implement them using code formatters and linters.

3.2 CODE STYLE AND TOOLING (ESLINT, PRETTIER, ETC.)

In the grand scheme of software development, code style and consistency might seem like minor details, but they are actually quite crucial for building robust, scalable, and collaborative applications. Just as a well-organized toolbox makes a carpenter more efficient, consistent code style and good tooling can make a development team much more productive, and improve the long-term maintainability of the application.

In this section, we'll delve into the importance of maintaining a consistent code style, and how to implement this using tools such as ESLint, Prettier, and more. We'll explore why these tools are essential and how they can be implemented to enhance code quality and team collaboration.

Why Does Code Style Matter?

Before we dive into the tools, it is essential to understand why consistent coding styles are important.

- **Readability:** Consistent code is easier to read. When all code follows the same style rules, it's much easier for developers to understand what's going on, reducing the cognitive load and making the codebase more accessible.
- **Maintainability:** Consistent code is easier to maintain. When you need to refactor or debug a code base that does not have style consistency, things can get really complicated, leading to mistakes and errors.
- **Collaboration:** When the entire team is following the same coding styles, it is easier to understand each others code, making collaboration much easier.
- **Reduced Bugs:** Enforcing consistent coding practices can prevent many errors from happening. Consistent code avoids inconsistencies, leading to fewer bugs.
- **Improved Productivity:** Consistent code allows developers to quickly jump between code sections, reduces friction, and improves overall productivity.

Think of code styles as a common language for your team. When you speak the same language, communication becomes effortless.

ESLint: Catching Errors and Enforcing Rules

ESLint is a powerful static analysis tool for JavaScript and TypeScript. It scans your code, looking for syntax errors, coding inconsistencies, and violations of best practices. ESLint is not a code formatter, but it can help you enforce many coding rules.

- **How it works:** ESLint parses your code, and highlights any potential errors or inconsistencies. You can customize the rules to your specific needs.
- **Benefits:** Identifies potential bugs early in the development process, enforces coding best practices, and improves the overall code quality.

Practical Implementation:

1. Install ESLint:

```
npm install eslint --save-dev
```

2. Create .eslintrc.json in your project root. Let's add some basic configurations.

```
{
"extends": ["eslint:recommended", "next/core-web-vitals"],
"rules": {
  "no-console": "warn",
  "no-unused-vars": "warn",
    "react/no-unescaped-entities": "off"
  }
}
```

This setup:

- extends: extends the recommended ESLint rules and the rules for Next.js projects.
- rules: defines some specific rules like marking console.log as a warning, marking unused variables as a warning, and disable the no-unescaped-entities rule for react.

1. Install the ESLint extension in your code editor. VSCode offers great ESLint support. Now you should see ESLint errors and warnings within your code editor as you code.

ESLint is an essential tool for any enterprise development team, it helps to improve code quality by detecting issues early.

Prettier: Code Formatting Made Easy

Prettier is an opinionated code formatter that automatically formats your code according to a set of rules. It helps to eliminate any inconsistencies, creating clean and consistent code.

- **How it works:** Prettier automatically reformats your code on save or on demand.
- **Benefits:** Eliminates inconsistencies, makes code more readable, and improves team collaboration.

Practical Implementation:

1. Install Prettier:

```
npm install prettier --save-dev
```

2. Create .prettierrc.json in your project root.

```
{
"semi": true,
"trailingComma": "all",
"singleQuote": true,
"printWidth": 100,
"tabWidth": 2
}
```

This configuration will ensure your code:

- Always ends with a semicolon
- Will add trailing commas at the end of each array, object, etc.

- Will prefer single quotes
- Will use 100 characters for print width
- Will use two spaces for tabs

3. Install the Prettier extension in your VSCode or your code editor.
4. Configure your code editor to format on save by adding this to your settings.json file:

```
"editor.formatOnSave": true,
"editor.defaultFormatter": "esbenp.prettier-vscode"
```

Now your code will be automatically formatted every time you save your code. You do not have to worry about formatting anymore.

Prettier makes code formatting easy, it improves code readability and saves you time.

Combining ESLint and Prettier

ESLint and Prettier work great together. ESLint focuses on catching errors, while Prettier focuses on formatting the code. By combining both tools, you can create a robust, consistent, and error-free code base.

Practical Implementation:

1. Add prettier to the ESLint extends list:

```
{
  "extends": ["eslint:recommended", "next/core-web-vitals",
"prettier"],
  "rules": {
    "no-console": "warn",
    "no-unused-vars": "warn",
    "react/no-unescaped-entities": "off"
  }
}
```

2. Install the VSCode code action extension:

```
npm install eslint-plugin-prettier eslint-config-
prettier --save-dev
```

3. Add this to your settings.json file:

```
"editor.codeActionsOnSave": {
  "source.fixAll.eslint": true
}
```

Now, every time you save your file, Prettier will format your code, and
ESLint will fix all fixable errors.

By combining both tools you will have a powerful way to improve your code
quality and code maintainability.

More Tools to Consider

There are other tools you may consider to help with code quality and
consistency:

- **Stylelint:** For styling, CSS, and Sass files.
- **Commitlint:** Enforce commit message conventions.
- **Husky:** To manage Git hooks.

Personal Insight

I've learned that a consistent code style and good tooling are not just about
aesthetics. They're a crucial part of building a successful enterprise
application. From personal experience, I remember joining teams where code
style was not enforced, and I was incredibly frustrated because I needed to
spend a lot of time understanding other people's code. Setting up tools early
in the project is a fantastic way to improve development velocity and code
maintainability.

Summary

Consistent code styles and tooling are the pillars of great code, it makes your
code easier to read, maintain, debug, and it helps your team to collaborate.
By setting up your tools and coding practices early in the process, you are
setting yourself for success.

In the next section we will discuss TypeScript and how to leverage it to improve your code quality.

3.3 TYPESCRIPT FOR ENHANCED TYPE SAFETY

In the world of JavaScript development, type errors are a common source of bugs and runtime headaches. As applications grow larger and more complex, managing these errors becomes increasingly challenging. This is where TypeScript steps in. TypeScript is a superset of JavaScript that adds static typing, helping you catch type-related errors during development instead of finding them in production.

In this section, we'll explore the benefits of TypeScript, how it enhances type safety, and how to practically implement it in your Next.js 15 project. Think of TypeScript as a reliable safety net that helps you build more robust and maintainable applications.

Why is Type Safety Important?

Before we jump into the specifics of TypeScript, let's discuss why type safety is essential:

- **Early Error Detection:** Typescript catches type related errors during compilation, allowing you to find them early in development, instead of in production.
- **Improved Code Quality:** Static typing makes the code more explicit, and increases readability, improving code quality.
- **Enhanced Maintainability:** Code with strong type definitions is easier to maintain and refactor, since you know what types to expect.
- **Better Collaboration:** When your code is well typed, your colleagues will know what to expect from a component or a function. This increases collaboration efficiency, and reduces ambiguity in development.
- **Reduced Runtime Errors:** Runtime errors can be hard to track, with TypeScript you are catching those errors during compile time, which will reduce the number of those errors, resulting in a more robust application.
- **Better Tooling Support:** TypeScript integrates well with code editors, offering intelligent autocompletion, type checking, and refactoring capabilities.

Type safety helps in preventing common errors that can lead to frustration, and production issues.

Key Features of TypeScript

TypeScript adds several powerful features to JavaScript:

- **Static Typing:** You explicitly define the types of your variables, functions, and objects.
- **Type Inference:** TypeScript can infer types without explicit annotations, making your code cleaner.
- **Interfaces and Types:** Define custom data structures and types.
- **Generics:** Create reusable components and functions that work with multiple types.
- **Type Annotations:** Add type definitions for variables, functions, objects, and interfaces.
- **Decorators:** Add metadata for classes and methods.

Practical Implementation: Getting Started

Since Next.js has first-class support for TypeScript, it was already included in your setup if you followed the steps in previous sections. If not, you can add it like this:

1. Install TypeScript:

```
npm install typescript @types/react @types/node --save-dev
```

2. Create a tsconfig.json file in your project root. Here is an example:

```
{
"compilerOptions": {
"target": "es5",
"lib": ["dom", "dom.iterable", "esnext"],
"allowJs": true,
"skipLibCheck": true,
"strict": true,
"forceConsistentCasingInFileNames": true,
"noEmit": true,
```

```
    "esModuleInterop": true,
    "module": "esnext",
    "moduleResolution": "node",
    "resolveJsonModule": true,
    "isolatedModules": true,
    "jsx": "preserve",
    "incremental": true,
        "baseUrl": ".",
        "paths": {
          "@/*": ["./src/*"]
        }
  },
  "include": ["next-env.d.ts", "**/*.ts", "**/*.tsx"],
  "exclude": ["node_modules"]
}
```

This configuration file defines how TypeScript compiles your code, and the rules that it should enforce.

3. Now, rename your javascript and jsx files to tsx or ts.

Now you are ready to start using TypeScript in your project.

Practical Implementation: Type Annotations

Let's explore a couple of practical examples.

1. In src/app/components/UserCard.tsx:

```
    interface UserProps {
  name: string;
  age: number;
  email: string;
}

const UserCard: React.FC<UserProps> = ({ name, age, email })
=> {
```

```
  return (
    <div className="user-card">
      <h2>{name}</h2>
      <p>Age: {age}</p>
      <p>Email: {email}</p>
    </div>
  );
};

export default UserCard;
```

Here we have defined an interface UserProps, which defines the shape of our component's properties. This ensures that the component receives the correct type of data.

2. In src/app/utils/api.ts:

```
  interface Post {
  userId: number,
  id: number,
  title: string,
  body: string
}

export async function fetchPosts(): Promise<Post[]> {
  const res = await
fetch('https://jsonplaceholder.typicode.com/posts');
  return await res.json();
}
```

Here we have defined a type for the object that will be returned by the fetchPosts API call. This makes it easier to work with the data as we have defined it as an array of type Post.

With these examples, TypeScript will show errors if you pass the wrong data type, avoiding runtime errors and helping you catch errors early in development.

Benefits of TypeScript in Enterprise Apps

- **Scalability:** Helps in building large, scalable applications that have good structure and are easy to maintain.
- **Maintainability:** TypeScript is easy to maintain, and is easy to onboard new developers as they can quickly see how the different pieces connect and what data types they should expect.
- **Reduced Bugs:** TypeScript detects bugs during development, reducing the number of runtime errors.
- **Better tooling:** TypeScript improves your developer experience, as most code editors offer rich tooling for TypeScript, improving productivity.

Personal Insight

From personal experience, adopting TypeScript has been a game changer. I've seen how it makes the code easier to read and to maintain, especially when working with a large team. The ability to catch errors during development has greatly improved the quality of the applications I have worked on. It requires a learning curve, but the benefits are immense.

Summary

TypeScript enhances type safety in your JavaScript projects and is an excellent addition to any project that needs to scale and be maintainable in the long run. By adopting TypeScript, you will write more robust and error-free code, which leads to a more enjoyable development experience.

In the next section, we will explore how to improve team collaboration with Git.

3.4 COLLABORATIVE GIT WORKFLOWS

In the world of software development, especially in enterprise settings, collaboration is the name of the game. Multiple developers working together on the same codebase can quickly become chaotic if not managed properly. This is where Git workflows come into play. Git workflows provide a structured way for teams to collaborate effectively, manage changes, and ensure code quality.

In this section, we'll explore why collaborative Git workflows are essential, different types of workflows, and how to implement a workflow that enhances your team's productivity and reduces conflicts. Think of Git workflows as a well-organized system of traffic rules that helps your team navigate the complexities of collaborative coding.

Why Are Git Workflows Essential?

Before we jump into the specifics, let's explore why establishing clear Git workflows is so important.

- **Collaboration:** A well-defined workflow ensures that multiple developers can work on the same codebase without causing chaos or introducing conflicts.
- **Version Control:** Git workflows allow you to track changes, manage versions, and revert to previous versions if necessary, giving you flexibility when things do not go as expected.
- **Code Quality:** Git workflows, such as the use of pull requests, ensure that code is reviewed before being merged, which leads to better quality code.
- **Reduced Conflicts:** A structured approach helps prevent merging conflicts that are difficult to resolve.
- **Scalability:** A good workflow scales with your application and team, ensuring you have a process in place for all changes.
- **Organization:** Keeps all changes organized, traceable, and understandable.

In the end, Git workflows help teams to work more efficiently and build high-quality applications.

Common Git Workflows

While there are many types of Git workflows, let's discuss the most common ones:

- **Feature Branch Workflow:** This is the most common workflow. Each new feature is developed in its own branch, which is merged into the main branch after review.

66

- **Gitflow Workflow:** This is more complex and has branches for features, releases, and hotfixes. It's suitable for large applications with a structured release process.
- **GitHub Flow:** A simplified version of Gitflow, ideal for smaller teams and applications with a continuous deployment process.

For most enterprise applications, the Feature Branch Workflow or the Gitflow Workflow is usually the best approach.

The Feature Branch Workflow: A Practical Approach

The Feature Branch Workflow is easy to adopt, and is suitable for most teams. It works as follows:

1. **Main Branch:** The main branch is the source of truth and should always contain the stable, production ready code.
2. **Develop Branch:** The develop branch is where new features are integrated. This is the branch to merge new pull requests.
3. **Feature Branches:** When you want to implement a new feature, you create a new branch from develop. The feature branch should have a name related to the feature you are working on, e.g. feature/new-login, or feat/implement-user-profile.
4. **Pull Requests:** After you are done with your changes, you create a pull request to merge the code from the feature branch into the develop branch.
5. **Code Reviews:** The pull request will be reviewed by your colleagues. Once it is approved, you can merge it to develop.
6. **Merge to Main:** When all tests have been passed, you can merge the develop branch into the main branch.

Practical Implementation:

Let's implement a feature using the Feature Branch Workflow:

1. Create a new feature branch:

```
git checkout -b feat/implement-user-profile
```

2. Make all your changes.
3. Add your changes:

```
git add .
```

4. Commit your changes:

```
git commit -m "feat: Implemented user profile feature"
```

5. Push to origin:

```
git push -u origin feat/implement-user-profile
```

6. Create a Pull Request: In GitHub, or GitLab, or BitBucket, create a Pull Request to merge the feat/implement-user-profile branch into the develop branch.
7. Review the code, and merge the Pull Request when it is approved.

Gitflow Workflow: A More Complex Approach

The Gitflow workflow is more complex, and has multiple branches such as:

- **Main:** Production ready code.
- **Develop:** New features are integrated here.
- **Feature Branches:** Branches for implementing new features.
- **Release Branches:** Used for preparing a new release.
- **Hotfix Branches:** Used for addressing critical bugs in the main branch.

While Gitflow is more complex, it is a solid choice for large projects that have a structured release process.

GitHub Flow: A Simpler Approach

The GitHub flow workflow is very similar to the Feature Branch Workflow, but it merges all code from the feature branch directly to the main branch, with no develop branch. It's a great approach for applications that are deployed often.

Best Practices for Collaborative Git Workflows

- **Commit Often:** Commit your code frequently with clear and descriptive commit messages.
- **Keep Branches Short-Lived:** Short-lived branches reduce the chance of conflicts.
- **Pull Requests are a Must:** Always use pull requests and code reviews to maintain code quality.
- **Code Review is Essential:** Do not merge your own code. Ask your peers to review it.
- **Rebase When Needed:** Rebase your feature branches before submitting a pull request. This keeps history tidy.
- **Stay Updated:** Always pull the latest changes to your branch before making changes.
- **Follow the process:** A defined Git workflow is nothing if the team is not following it. All team members should follow the process.

Personal Insight

From personal experience, a good Git workflow is indispensable for team productivity and code quality. I have worked on projects where developers did not use pull requests or code reviews, and the number of bugs that ended in production were really frustrating. By implementing a structured process, we managed to dramatically improve code quality and delivery velocity.

Summary

By implementing a well-defined Git workflow, your team will be able to work collaboratively and efficiently. Choosing the right Git workflow will improve code quality, minimize conflicts, and create a more enjoyable development experience.

In the next section, we will discuss environment variables and how to manage them across different environments.

3.5 MANAGING ENVIRONMENT VARIABLES ACROSS ENVIRONMENTS

In the world of software development, applications often need different configurations for different environments. You might have different API endpoints for your development, staging, and production environments. You might use a different database, or a different authentication provider. These configurations shouldn't be hardcoded into the application. This is where environment variables come into play. Environment variables allow you to configure your applications externally, adapting them to each environment without requiring changes to the code.

In this section, we'll discuss why managing environment variables is important, how to use them in Next.js 15, and some best practices. Think of environment variables as flexible settings that let you adapt your application to different contexts, like adjusting the settings of a machine based on the specific task.

Why Are Environment Variables Important?

Before we dive into the specifics of implementation, it is important to understand why environment variables are so important.

- **Configuration Management:** Environment variables are the standard for managing configuration in different environments (development, staging, production).
- **Security:** They help in securely managing sensitive information like API keys, database passwords, and secrets by keeping them outside the codebase.
- **Flexibility:** They allow you to easily configure your application for different scenarios without making changes to your code.
- **Maintainability:** Environment variables keep code clean by removing environment-specific values.
- **Collaboration:** Different developers can use different configurations locally without conflicts.

In short, environment variables help improve the security, flexibility, and maintainability of your application.

How to Manage Environment Variables in Next.js 15

Next.js 15 has built-in support for environment variables, making it easy to use them in your application.

- **.env Files:** You can create different .env files for different environments.
  - o .env.local: Used for local development.
  - o .env.development: Used for the development environment.
  - o .env.production: Used for the production environment.

These files contain your environment variables in a key-value format, such as:

```
NEXT_PUBLIC_API_URL=https://api.example.com
DATABASE_URL=postgres://user:password@host:5432/database
SECRET_KEY=your_secret_key
```

- **Accessing Environment Variables:** You can access environment variables in your application using process.env.

Practical Implementation:

Let's see how you can implement environment variables in your project.

1. Create the following files in the root of your project:
   - .env.local
   - .env.development
   - .env.production
2. In .env.local, set up your variables:

```
NEXT_PUBLIC_API_URL=http://localhost:3000/api
```

.

3. In .env.development, set up your variables:

```
NEXT_PUBLIC_API_URL=https://dev.example.com/api
```

4. In .env.production, set up your variables:

```
NEXT_PUBLIC_API_URL=https://prod.example.com/api
```

In this example, we set up different API URLs for each environment.

5. Access your variable in a component. In src/app/components/ApiCall.tsx:

```
      async function fetchMyData() {
   const apiUrl = process.env.NEXT_PUBLIC_API_URL;
   const res = await fetch(`${apiUrl}/users`);
   return res.json();
}


const ApiCall = async () => {
    const data = await fetchMyData()


    return (
        <div>
            <h1>Users</h1>
            {data.map(user => <p
key={user.id}>{user.name}</p>)}
        </div>
    )
}
export default ApiCall
```

Here, the NEXT_PUBLIC_API_URL variable is used to create the API URL based on the current environment.

Important Considerations

- **NEXT_PUBLIC_ Prefix:** Environment variables prefixed with NEXT_PUBLIC_ are exposed to the browser. You should not store any sensitive data in these variables. Any variables that are not prefixed with NEXT_PUBLIC_ are only available on the server.
- **Sensitive Information:** You should never store sensitive information in files that are version controlled (such as .env files).
- **Environment Variables in Production:** Environment variables in production are usually configured differently depending on your hosting provider.

Best Practices for Managing Environment Variables

- **Use .env.local for Local Development:** Keep all local configurations in the .env.local file. This file is not version controlled.
- **Use Different Files for Different Environments:** Use different .env files for each environment.
- **Avoid Committing .env Files:** .env files should never be added to your Git repository. Use .gitignore to exclude them.
- **Centralize Your Configurations:** Keep all of your environment variables well organized to avoid confusion and reduce human errors.
- **Use a Secret Manager:** For production environments, it is better to store sensitive information in a secret manager provided by your cloud provider.

Personal Insight

I've learned from hard experience that keeping sensitive information in code can lead to security problems. Setting up a consistent and reliable environment variable strategy is a must for enterprise applications. Using environment variables allows for better flexibility, security and maintainability of applications. I have also learned that keeping environment variables organized is just as important. A good system will reduce the chance of human errors.

Summary

Managing environment variables across environments is a fundamental part of building enterprise applications. You can easily create flexible, secure, and maintainable applications by following the recommended practices in this section.

In the next section, we will explore CI/CD and how you can automate your deployments.

3.6 CI/CD FUNDAMENTALS FOR AUTOMATED DEPLOYMENT

In the fast-paced world of software development, deploying code manually is a thing of the past. It's slow, error-prone, and frankly, quite tedious. That's where Continuous Integration and Continuous Deployment (CI/CD) come into play. CI/CD pipelines automate the process of building, testing, and deploying your code, ensuring that new changes are integrated, tested, and released quickly and reliably.

In this section, we'll explore what CI/CD is, why it's essential, and how to set up a basic CI/CD pipeline for your Next.js 15 application. Think of CI/CD as an automated factory that takes your code, puts it through a series of checks, and then delivers the finished product to your users.

What is CI/CD?

Before we dive into the specifics of setting up a pipeline, it's important to understand the core concepts:

- **Continuous Integration (CI):** CI focuses on frequently merging code changes from multiple developers into a shared repository. The CI process automatically builds and tests code every time changes are pushed, allowing developers to catch integration errors early.
- **Continuous Deployment (CD):** CD takes things a step further by automatically deploying code to the production environment or other target environments after it has passed the tests. This ensures that new features and bug fixes are released frequently and reliably.

CI and CD usually go hand in hand, creating a streamlined workflow for the entire development cycle.

Why Is CI/CD Essential?

Let's discuss the benefits of implementing a CI/CD pipeline:

- **Faster Release Cycles:** Automated deployment enables quicker release cycles, as the process of deployment is very quick.
- **Reduced Human Error:** Automating the process reduces errors as the code is not manually moved from one environment to another.
- **Improved Code Quality:** Automated testing helps to catch errors early in the development cycle, before they are deployed to production.
- **Increased Productivity:** CI/CD pipelines free developers from manual tasks, allowing them to focus on writing code instead.
- **Faster Feedback Loops:** CI/CD allows developers to quickly see their changes in a live environment, reducing the feedback loops and reducing the time to production.

- **Consistency:** A CI/CD pipeline ensures that each deployment follows the same steps, which prevents inconsistent and buggy releases.
- **Rollbacks:** Automated processes make it much easier to quickly roll back a buggy release, preventing extended downtime.

CI/CD is a necessary component of any enterprise application, as it provides a structured way to make your deployments smooth, reliable, and scalable.

CI/CD Pipeline Fundamentals

A typical CI/CD pipeline includes the following stages:

1. **Source Code Management:** Changes are pushed to a version control system, such as Git.
2. **Build:** The code is compiled and packaged, creating deployable artifacts.
3. **Test:** Automated tests are run to verify that the new changes are working as expected.
4. **Deploy:** If all tests pass, the code is automatically deployed to the production environment.
5. **Monitor:** After deployment, the application is monitored for any errors or issues.

Setting Up a CI/CD Pipeline for Next.js 15

Let's explore a simplified CI/CD pipeline using GitHub Actions and Vercel. GitHub actions will be used for the CI part, and Vercel will be used for deployment.

1. **Configure Vercel:** Create a Vercel account, and link your repository to Vercel.
2. **Create a GitHub Actions Workflow:** Create a file in .github/workflows/main.yaml in your repository with the following content:

```
name: CI/CD Pipeline

on:
  push:
    branches:
```

```
      - develop

jobs:
  build:
    runs-on: ubuntu-latest
    steps:
      - uses: actions/checkout@v3
      - uses: actions/setup-node@v3
        with:
          node-version: 18
      - run: npm ci
      - run: npm run build
  deploy:
    needs: build
    runs-on: ubuntu-latest
    steps:
      - name: Deploy to Vercel
        uses: amondnet/vercel-action@v20
        with:
          vercel-token: ${{ secrets.VERCEL_TOKEN }}
          vercel-org-id: ${{ secrets.VERCEL_ORG_ID }}
          vercel-project-id: ${{
secrets.VERCEL_PROJECT_ID }}
```

Let's break down this configuration:

- o name: Specifies the name of the workflow.
- o on: Specifies that this workflow runs every time a change is pushed to the develop branch.
- o jobs: Defines the jobs that will be performed during the workflow.
  - build: This job checks out the code, installs node, installs dependencies, and builds the application.
  - deploy: This job deploys the application using the Vercel action. You will need to create the secrets in your repository. You can find the variables in Vercel.

With this basic configuration, every time you push changes to the develop branch, the code will be built and deployed automatically using GitHub Actions and Vercel.

Important Considerations

- **Testing:** While this example has a simple build step, you will want to add integration and unit tests to make sure your application is working correctly.
- **Environment Variables:** Make sure to properly set up environment variables in your CI/CD pipeline, based on your environment.
- **Secrets:** Protect API keys and other sensitive information using secrets management tools offered by your CI/CD provider.
- **Rollbacks:** You need to have a strategy in place for rolling back deployments. Many CI/CD providers offer rollback functionalities.
- **Monitoring:** Make sure to set up monitoring to ensure your application is working well.

Different Deployment Strategies

There are many deployment strategies you can adopt, depending on your needs:

- **Blue/Green Deployments:** Run a new version of your application alongside the old version. Once the new version is tested, you switch all traffic to the new version.
- **Canary Deployments:** Roll out your new application to a subset of users, testing the performance and functionality, before rolling it to all users.
- **Rolling Deployments:** Update your application gradually, by deploying new versions to a small subset of servers.

Personal Insight

I've learned that setting up a reliable CI/CD pipeline is crucial for building enterprise applications. Manual deployments are frustrating, error-prone, and slow. By setting up an automated deployment process, your development cycle will dramatically improve, and you will free up developers to focus on more important things. I also find that setting up a monitoring system is key to detect any issues with the deployed application, which allows you to react quickly in case of problems.

Summary

By implementing a robust CI/CD pipeline, you can automate your build, test, and deploy processes, leading to faster, more reliable, and higher-quality application releases. This automation is a must for any enterprise-level application.

In the next chapter, we'll start exploring application architecture and how to create scalable enterprise applications.

PART 2: ARCHITECTING FOR SCALABILITY AND PERFORMANCE

CHAPTER 4: DESIGNING SCALABLE APPLICATION ARCHITECTURES

Alright, we've established the foundations for building enterprise-level applications, focusing on tooling, workflows, and core Next.js concepts. Now, let's zoom out and consider the overall architecture of our applications. A well-designed architecture is crucial for building scalable, maintainable, and robust systems. It's not just about getting the code to work; it's about designing a system that can grow and evolve with your business needs.

In this chapter, we'll explore different architectural patterns, focusing on how to implement them effectively in Next.js 15. We'll discuss the pros and cons of monoliths vs. microservices, the benefits of domain-driven design, and practical strategies for building scalable applications. This will be your guide to planning and building a flexible, maintainable system.

4.1 MONOLITHS VS. MICROSERVICES: CHOOSING THE RIGHT APPROACH

When embarking on a new software project, one of the most fundamental architectural decisions you'll face is whether to build a monolith or a microservices architecture. It's a bit like deciding whether to build a single, multi-functional building or a complex of smaller, specialized buildings. Each approach has its own strengths and weaknesses, and the "right" choice is heavily dependent on the specifics of your project.

In this section, we'll unpack the differences between monolithic and microservices architectures, weigh their pros and cons, and guide you in selecting the most suitable approach for your specific project needs. This is about strategy, and recognizing the benefits and drawbacks of each architectural approach.

Understanding the Monolithic Architecture

The monolithic architecture is the traditional way of building applications. Imagine a single, large application where all the code, business logic, UI components, and database interactions are tightly coupled. It's like having one single large building, with all functions within it.

- **How It Works:** All parts of the application are bundled into a single code base.
- **Deployment:** The entire application is deployed as a single unit.
- **Communication:** Components communicate directly with each other within the same application.

Pros of a Monolithic Architecture:

- **Simplicity:** Monoliths are generally easier to develop, deploy, and manage, especially in the early stages of a project. There is less infrastructure needed, and it is simpler to get started.
- **Performance:** In certain scenarios, a monolith can outperform microservices because there's no network overhead for communication between components.
- **Easy Debugging:** When all code is in one place, it's often easier to debug and trace issues.
- **Easier Testing:** Testing a monolithic application can be simpler since you're dealing with one single unit.
- **Lower Operational Overhead:** A monolith requires less infrastructure management than a microservices architecture, making it easier for smaller teams to operate.
- **Straightforward Refactoring:** Refactoring is often simpler, as changes are contained within a single code base.

Cons of a Monolithic Architecture:

- **Scalability Challenges:** Scaling a monolith can be difficult because you need to scale all components together, even if only one part of the application needs more resources.
- **Deployment Bottlenecks:** Deploying changes can be slow because you need to deploy the entire application, even if the changes are small.
- **Maintenance Complexity:** As the codebase grows, it can become more complex to maintain, making it harder to add new features and fix bugs.
- **Technology Lock-in:** Monoliths can make it difficult to adopt new technologies as the entire codebase might need a major overhaul.
- **Single Point of Failure:** If one component fails in a monolith, the entire application can be impacted.
- **Slower Development Velocity:** As the team grows, and the codebase becomes larger, development becomes slower.

Understanding the Microservices Architecture

The microservices architecture takes a different approach. It's like creating a network of small, specialized buildings that work together. Each building (microservice) performs a specific function and communicates with the others via APIs.

- **How It Works:** Applications are broken into small, independent services, each responsible for a specific feature.
- **Deployment:** Each service is deployed separately.
- **Communication:** Services communicate through APIs.

Pros of a Microservices Architecture:

- **Scalability:** Each microservice can be scaled independently, allowing for better resource utilization and scalability.
- **Technology Diversity:** Different services can use different technologies, allowing you to choose the right tool for each job.
- **Maintainability:** Each service is small and focused, making it easier to develop, test, deploy, and maintain.
- **Faster Development Cycles:** As services are independent, changes can be made, tested, and released independently, improving development velocity.
- **Resiliency:** If one microservice fails, the rest of the application can continue to function, enhancing fault tolerance.

Cons of a Microservices Architecture:

- **Increased Complexity:** Microservices introduce more complexity in the areas of architecture, development, deployment, and operations.
- **Operational Overhead:** Requires more infrastructure and management to handle multiple services.
- **Debugging Challenges:** Debugging a microservices application is complex due to its distributed nature.
- **Communication Overhead:** Inter-service communication introduces network overhead, making some operations slower.
- **Data Consistency:** Managing data consistency across different services is difficult.
- **Security:** Securing a distributed system can be complex.

Choosing the Right Approach: A Strategic Decision

Choosing between a monolith and microservices isn't a one-size-fits-all decision. It depends on various factors, such as the size of your project, your team, and your long-term goals.

- **Startups and Small Projects:** For startups or small projects, starting with a monolith is usually a good idea due to its simplicity and speed of development.
- **Large Applications with Complex Requirements:** Microservices are a good option for large, complex applications with diverse needs, and large development teams.
- **Teams with Different Skillsets:** If your team has diverse skillsets, you can leverage microservices to allow people to use the technologies they are familiar with.
- **Scalability is Critical:** If scalability is critical, you should probably consider microservices.
- **Long-term Maintainability:** Microservices provide better maintainability in the long run.
- **Flexibility:** If flexibility is important, microservices are better, since they allow you to chose the right technology for each scenario.

Practical Implementation:

There isn't a simple code example to demonstrate monolithic versus microservices. It is not code, but an architectural decision. However, let's look at an example of the difference:

1. **Monolith:** In a monolithic application, all of the following functionalities reside inside the same application: User management, product catalog, order management, payment processing, and analytics. Each of the modules would call each other using function calls. This approach is simple, but has all the limitations discussed above.
2. **Microservices:** In a microservices architecture, each of the functionalities mentioned above (user management, product catalog, etc), will reside on their own service. These services will then call each other using APIs, or other mechanisms. This allows for each service to be scaled independently.

The right choice depends on your requirements, and you must be ready to adapt to the specific needs of your project.

My Personal Experience

I've been involved in projects using both architectures and have come to understand that there's no universal "best" approach. I find that monolithic architectures can be suitable for most starting projects, however, as the project grows in complexity, and team size grows, a migration to microservices is probably going to be the best approach. It's important to consider your goals, and the context of your specific project.

In Summary

Choosing between a monolithic and microservices architecture is a critical decision. By weighing the pros and cons of each approach, and analyzing your team's and project's requirements, you'll be better prepared to make the right choice, which will have a huge impact on your application's success.

In the next section, we'll explore Domain Driven Design, a design approach that can be used in both monolithic and microservices architectures.

4.2 DOMAIN-DRIVEN DESIGN FOR COMPLEX APPLICATIONS

When building complex software systems, especially in the enterprise space, it's easy to get lost in the technical weeds. You start thinking about databases, APIs, and user interfaces, sometimes forgetting the core purpose of the software: to solve real business problems. This is where Domain-Driven Design (DDD) comes in. DDD is not a technology, or a framework, but a philosophy that guides you to model software based on the complexities of the business domain.

In this section, we'll explore the core principles of Domain-Driven Design, why it's beneficial for complex applications, and how to apply DDD concepts in your Next.js 15 projects. Think of DDD as a roadmap that helps you align your technical implementation with the business needs, ensuring that your software solves the right problems in the right way.

What is Domain-Driven Design?

Domain-Driven Design is an approach to developing software based on the real-world business domain it is trying to solve. It's not a set of rules or a framework, but rather a set of principles that emphasize:

- **Ubiquitous Language:** Creating a common language between developers and business experts.
- **Domain Modeling:** Focusing on understanding the business domain and translating that understanding into the software model.
- **Bounded Contexts:** Defining clear boundaries for different parts of the system, each with its own model and logic.
- **Strategic Design:** Focusing on the core domain, and creating a plan based on business value.
- **Tactical Design:** Using specific patterns and techniques for the actual implementation of the domain.

These elements guide the development process to create a system that accurately represents the domain that it is trying to solve.

Why is DDD Important for Complex Applications?

In complex applications, it's easy to lose sight of the core business logic, which leads to software that does not truly represent the business needs. DDD helps in:

- **Aligning Technology with Business:** DDD aligns software development with the business needs. It helps to create a system that meets the business objectives.
- **Improved Communication:** By establishing a ubiquitous language, DDD facilitates communication between business experts and developers, reducing misunderstandings.
- **Better Modularity:** DDD encourages you to break the system into bounded contexts, each with its own model and logic, resulting in better organization.
- **Scalability:** The use of bounded contexts makes the application more scalable, as each context is relatively independent.
- **Reduced Complexity:** By focusing on the domain model, it helps to reduce the complexity of the application by separating it into different bounded contexts.
- **Increased Agility:** Because the application is modeled on the business domain, it makes it easier to adapt to new business requirements.

In summary, DDD helps in creating more business-focused, maintainable and flexible applications.

Core Concepts of Domain-Driven Design

Let's explore some key concepts in DDD:

- **Ubiquitous Language:** This is a shared vocabulary used by both developers and business experts. This helps with better communication, and ensures that everyone is using the same language. For example, instead of talking about users and profiles you may use customers in your business, so you would use customers in your code.
- **Domain Model:** The domain model is a conceptual model that reflects the key concepts of the business domain. It contains domain entities, aggregates, and value objects. The domain model is the heart of your application.
- **Bounded Contexts:** In large applications, you may have many subdomains. Bounded contexts define the boundaries of each subdomain. Each bounded context is isolated and has its own model and logic.
- **Entities:** Entities are objects that have a unique identity, that can be tracked across different operations. For example, a user, a product, or an order.
- **Value Objects:** Value objects are objects that do not have a unique identity, and are identified by its properties. For example, addresses, or phone numbers.
- **Aggregates:** Aggregates are clusters of entities and value objects that are treated as a single unit for data consistency purposes. For example, a product and its description can be an aggregate.
- **Domain Events:** These are events that occur within a domain that are relevant to the business. For example, an order being created, or a user being registered.
- **Repositories:** Repositories are data access layers that encapsulate the logic to access data from the underlying data store.
- **Domain Services:** Domain services are operations that do not belong to any entity or value object but are part of the business logic. For example, an email service.

Practical Implementation in a Next.js 15 Project

Let's illustrate how to apply some DDD concepts in a Next.js project. Imagine you're building an e-commerce platform.

1. **Ubiquitous Language:**

- o Instead of calling them "users", the business experts call them "customers". Therefore, in your code you will use Customer, instead of User.
- o You will call products items.

2. **Bounded Contexts:**
   - o You can have an order bounded context, which includes everything related to orders (entities, aggregates, domain events, and repositories), and a product bounded context.
   - o This helps keep related logic separate and improves the structure of the application.

3. **Domain Entities:**
   - o Create an entity to represent a Product in src/domain/product/entities/product.ts:

```
interface ProductProps {
  id: string;
  name: string;
  description: string;
  price: number;
}


class Product {
  id: string;
  name: string;
  description: string;
  price: number;

  constructor({id, name, description, price}: ProductProps) {
    this.id = id;
    this.name = name;
    this.description = description;
    this.price = price;
  }
}
export default Product
```

4. **Value Objects**

- o Create a value object to represent an Address in src/domain/order/value-objects/address.ts:

```
interface AddressProps {
  street: string;
  city: string;
  zipCode: string;
}
class Address {
  street: string;
  city: string;
  zipCode: string;
  constructor({street, city, zipCode}: AddressProps) {
    this.street = street;
    this.city = city;
    this.zipCode = zipCode;
  }
}
export default Address
```

5. **Domain Service**
   - o Create a service to send emails in src/domain/shared/services/email-service.ts:

```
interface EmailProps {
  to: string;
  subject: string;
  body: string;
}
const sendEmail = async ({ to, subject, body }: EmailProps) => {
  //email sending logic
}
export default sendEmail
```

6. **Repositories:**

- Create an interface to fetch products in src/domain/product/repositories/product-repository.ts:

```
import Product from '../entities/product'
    interface ProductRepository {
        getProducts(): Promise<Product[]>
        getProductById(id:string): Promise<Product>
    }
export default ProductRepository
```

- Create a concrete class that implement ProductRepository in src/app/adapters/product-repository.ts

```
import Product from '@/src/domain/product/entities/product'
import ProductRepository from
'@/src/domain/product/repositories/product-repository'


class ProductRepositoryImpl implements ProductRepository {
    async getProducts() : Promise<Product[]> {
        const res = await
fetch('https://fakestoreapi.com/products');
        return res.json()
    }
    async getProductById(id: string): Promise<Product> {
        const res = await
fetch(`https://fakestoreapi.com/products/${id}`);
        return res.json()
    }
}


export default ProductRepositoryImpl
```

With this example, we have started implementing our domain layer with a couple of examples: Entities, Value Objects, Domain Services, and Repositories.

My Experience

In my experience, DDD is a great way to approach complex applications. When you start thinking of your code based on the business needs, you start building a system that is closer to the business needs, reducing misunderstanding, and reducing complexity. DDD is a game changer in how I develop applications.

Summary

Domain-Driven Design helps to build applications that are aligned with your business needs, improves communication, and produces code that is easier to understand, maintain, and evolve. By adopting DDD you will improve the way that your code is modeled, improving flexibility and maintainability.

In the next section, we will explore how to build modular and reusable components.

4.3 BUILDING MODULAR AND REUSABLE COMPONENTS

In the realm of software development, particularly when building large, complex applications, the ability to write modular and reusable components is a critical skill. It's a bit like building with Lego bricks instead of crafting each piece from scratch – you assemble your application from well-defined, reusable building blocks, which makes the development process much more efficient, maintainable, and enjoyable.

In this section, we'll explore why modular and reusable components are essential, how they contribute to scalability and maintainability, and how you can create effective reusable components in your Next.js 15 applications. This is about efficiency and creating code that is easy to test, maintain, and scale.

Why Are Modular and Reusable Components Important?

Before we dive into the specifics, let's discuss why building modular and reusable components is so important:

- **Reduced Code Duplication:** Reusing components means you don't have to write the same code repeatedly, which reduces the size of your code base.

- **Improved Maintainability:** When you need to fix or update a component, you only need to change it in one place, and the changes are propagated everywhere it is used.
- **Increased Productivity:** When you reuse existing components, you do not have to code the same functionality from scratch, which improves development speed.
- **Consistency:** Reusable components help create a consistent look and feel throughout the application, improving user experience.
- **Better Testability:** Reusable components are easier to test as you can test it in isolation, and it improves overall code quality.
- **Scalability:** Building applications with modular, reusable components makes it easier to scale the application, as you can easily add new features without disrupting the existing ones.

In the end, modular and reusable components are the foundation for creating efficient, scalable, and maintainable applications.

Principles of Creating Reusable Components

Let's look at some guidelines to build effective reusable components:

- **Single Responsibility:** Components should focus on one specific task, making them easier to understand and reuse.
- **Abstracted Functionality:** Components should not depend on specific implementations or external logic, they should depend on abstractions.
- **Clear API:** Components should have well-defined and clear interfaces, with clear properties and outputs.
- **Configurability:** Components should be configurable through their properties, allowing to reuse them in different scenarios.
- **Testable:** Components should be easy to test in isolation, ensuring that they work as expected.
- **Documented:** Components should be well documented for other developers to understand how to use them effectively.

Practical Implementation in Next.js 15

Let's walk through creating a few reusable components in a Next.js application.

1. **Reusable Button Component:**
    o   Create src/app/components/Button.tsx:

```
    interface ButtonProps {
  children: React.ReactNode;
  onClick?: () => void;
  type?: 'button' | 'submit' | 'reset';
  className?: string
}


const Button: React.FC<ButtonProps> = ({ children, onClick,
type = 'button', className = '' }) => {
    return (
    <button className={`bg-blue-500 hover:bg-blue-700 text-
white py-2 px-4 rounded ${className}`}
            onClick={onClick} type={type}>
      {children}
    </button>
  );
};
export default Button;
```

This button component is generic, it uses children to specify
the text in the button, an onClick callback to handle the button
click, and type for the button type. It also has a className
parameter, that allows for extra customization. This
component is reusable and can be used across your
application.

- Usage:

```
import Button from './components/Button';


export default function MyPage() {
  return (
    <div>
        <Button onClick={() => console.log("Button
clicked")}>Click Me</Button>
    </div>
    );
```

```
}
```

2. **Reusable Card Component:**
   o Create src/app/components/Card.tsx:

```
    interface CardProps {
  title: string;
  content: React.ReactNode
  className?: string
}


const Card: React.FC<CardProps> = ({ title, content,
className = '' }) => {
    return (
        <div className={`p-4 bg-white shadow-md rounded-md
${className}`}>
            <h2 className="text-xl font-bold mb-
2">{title}</h2>
            <div>{content}</div>
        </div>
    );
};
export default Card;
```

   o Usage:

```
    import Card from './components/Card';


export default function MyPage() {
    return(
    <Card title="My Card" content={<p>This is my card
content</p>} />
    )
}
```

This component shows that components can contain other components and content, increasing reusability.

3. **Reusable Input Component:**
   o Create src/app/components/Input.tsx:

```
interface InputProps {
label: string
 placeholder?: string
 type?: string
 value: string
 onChange: (value: string) => void
 name: string
}
const Input: React.FC<InputProps> = ({ label, placeholder,
type = 'text', value, onChange, name }) => {
    return (
        <div>
            <label htmlFor={name}>{label}</label>
            <input placeholder={placeholder} value={value}
onChange={(e) => onChange(e.target.value)} type={type}
name={name}/>
        </div>
    )
}
export default Input
```

   o Usage:

```
import Input from "./components/Input";
import {useState} from "react";

export default function MyPage() {
    const [inputValue, setInputValue] = useState("")
    return (
        <div>
```

```
        <Input label="My Input" name="myinput"
type="text" value={inputValue} onChange={setInputValue}/>
        </div>
    )
  }
```

This component allows you to create any type of input.

These examples illustrate how to create reusable components by keeping them generic, configurable, and focused on a specific task. You can create more components based on your needs.

My Experience

I've come to realize that building applications with reusable components is crucial for maintaining consistency and improving productivity. Once you have a library of reusable components, development speed dramatically increases, and you start seeing the benefits of the effort you have put into it. I always emphasize to the teams that I work with to focus on creating reusable components.

Summary

Building modular and reusable components is a must for enterprise applications. This approach saves time, reduces errors, makes it easier to maintain code, and makes the development process more enjoyable.

In the next section, we will discuss component libraries and design systems.

4.4 COMPONENT LIBRARIES AND DESIGN SYSTEMS

Building large-scale applications, especially in the enterprise world, requires a robust and consistent approach to user interface design. It's not enough to create individual, isolated components; you need a way to ensure that all parts of your application adhere to a unified style and functionality. This is where component libraries and design systems come in. They are the secret ingredients for scaling design and ensuring a consistent user experience.

In this section, we'll explore what component libraries and design systems are, how they differ, and how they can benefit your development workflow. Think of component libraries and design systems as a shared language and a common toolkit that empowers development teams to build cohesive and high-quality user interfaces.

What are Component Libraries?

A component library is a collection of reusable UI components that can be used across different parts of an application. These components are designed to be generic and configurable, allowing developers to quickly assemble user interfaces without writing code from scratch. A component library is, in essence, a well organized toolbox for building consistent UI.

- **Focus:** Primarily on reusable UI elements (buttons, inputs, cards, etc.)
- **Scope:** Usually limited to the components themselves, without comprehensive guidelines on usage.
- **Implementation:** It's usually implemented in a specific technology (e.g., React, Vue, etc.)

Benefits of Component Libraries:

- **Faster Development:** Developers can quickly build UIs by reusing existing components.
- **Consistency:** Helps maintain a consistent look and feel throughout the application.
- **Maintainability:** Updates and bug fixes to components are propagated everywhere, reducing maintenance time.
- **Code Reusability:** Prevents code duplication and promotes the reusability of UI elements.
- **Improved Productivity:** Speeds up development by providing components that are ready to use.
- **Scalability:** Makes it easier to scale your application.

What are Design Systems?

A design system is more comprehensive than a component library. It includes not only UI components but also design principles, style guides, usage guidelines, and documentation. A design system is a living document that evolves with the needs of the application. It is in essence a shared language, and a way of thinking about design.

- **Focus:** On the overall design language and user experience. It also includes components, guidelines, style, branding and more.
- **Scope:** Broader than just components, it includes the rationale behind design choices, brand guidelines, and accessibility rules.
- **Implementation:** Usually technology agnostic. Although they can be implemented using a technology (e.g. React components), the principles, guidelines, and style can be applied across different technologies.

Benefits of Design Systems:

- **Consistency:** Guarantees consistency across the whole organization, improving user experience.
- **Scalability:** Helps scale the application, as developers know how to build new components.
- **Collaboration:** Provides a shared language and reference for both designers and developers.
- **Efficiency:** Speeds up the development and design processes.
- **Accessibility:** Often includes accessibility standards and guidelines, which creates more accessible applications.
- **Improved Branding:** Helps reinforce the brand's style, which ensures that the brand identity is consistent.
- **Cost Savings:** Reduces development costs in the long term as you have established a system in place to develop new components and features.

Component Libraries vs. Design Systems: Key Differences

Feature	Component Library	Design System
Focus	Reusable UI elements	Overall design language and user experience
Scope	Components themselves	Components, guidelines, style, branding, etc.
Purpose	Provides reusable UI parts	Provides a complete framework for design and development
Documentation	Limited to component usage	Extensive, including design principles

Practical Implementation: Setting Up a Basic Component Library

While creating a full-blown design system is outside the scope of this book, let's walk through creating a basic component library that you can expand upon:

1. **Project Setup:** In your Next.js project, you already have the src/app/components directory. This is a good starting point.
2. **Organize Your Components:** Create a folder for each set of components, so you can group related components.

```
    src/
  app/
    components/
       button/
          Button.tsx
       input/
          Input.tsx
       card/
         Card.tsx
       layout/
          Header.tsx
          Footer.tsx
```

3. **Implement Components:** You can use the examples of the Button, Card, and Input in the previous section. Here is an example for Header:

```
const Header = () => {
  return (
      <header className="bg-gray-800 text-white p-4">
         <h1>My Application Header</h1>
      </header>
  )
}
export default Header
```

4. **Document Components:** Provide basic documentation for your components in the code itself, and add a README.md file to each directory with guidelines and examples of usage.
5. **Centralize styles:** You can create a file with all the css styles you use in the component library to ensure consistency.

This approach creates a simple, yet scalable way to implement a component library.

Using an Existing Design System or Component Library

If you don't want to create your own library from scratch, you can leverage existing libraries and design systems:

- **Tailwind CSS:** A utility-first CSS framework, it doesn't include a set of components, but it includes styles, and you can quickly build your own components.
- **Chakra UI:** A component library that includes accessibility features, and components that are ready to use.
- **MUI (Material UI):** A large set of components based on Material Design.
- **Ant Design:** A powerful enterprise design system with a lot of components and customization options.

These libraries offer a fantastic starting point for building your application's user interface.

Personal Insight

From my personal experience, a solid component library or a design system is a must for large teams working on complex applications. I have seen how it creates consistency and productivity. Creating a design system might be a complex task, but the long term benefits are significant. Even if you start small, it's worth investing time to create your own library or adopt an existing one.

Summary

Component libraries and design systems are essential for building scalable and maintainable applications, especially in large enterprise teams. By implementing a component library or adopting a design system, you will create a more consistent user experience, accelerate development, and improve collaboration.

In the next section, we'll explore advanced techniques for managing state in large, complex applications.

4.5 ADVANCED STATE MANAGEMENT AT SCALE

In the journey of building enterprise applications, managing application state effectively is paramount. As your application grows in size and complexity, simply relying on component-level state becomes impractical. This is where advanced state management solutions come into play. It's like having a central control room for your application, where you can easily manage the different parts, and ensure they are in sync.

In this section, we'll explore the challenges of managing state in large applications, and introduce some of the most popular state management tools available in React. We will also explore the pros and cons of each solution. This is about maintaining the flow of data in your application, ensuring consistency, scalability, and maintainability.

The Challenge of State Management

Before we delve into specific tools, let's discuss why state management becomes a challenge in larger applications:

- **Complexity:** As your application grows, state becomes more complex. You have many components sharing state, which can become hard to track.
- **Prop Drilling:** Passing data down multiple layers of components can be inefficient and tedious, and can be difficult to maintain.
- **Data Inconsistency:** Without a central source of truth, it's easy for data to become inconsistent across different parts of your application, leading to bugs.
- **Difficulty in Testing:** Components that depend on prop drilling are often harder to test as the state is tied to a very specific component hierarchy.
- **Performance Bottlenecks:** Poorly managed state can result in performance issues, especially with complex data and frequent updates.

To prevent these challenges, you need a robust state management solution that can handle the complexities of large-scale applications.

Options for Advanced State Management

Here are some of the most popular state management libraries you might want to consider for your projects:

1. **React Context API:**
   - **How it Works:** A built-in React feature that allows you to share state across multiple components without prop drilling.
   - **Use Cases:** Simple to medium complexity applications. Good for application-wide states (theme, authentication, user settings).
   - **Pros:** Built into React, it is easy to use, and it doesn't add extra dependencies to your project.
   - **Cons:** Not ideal for complex data and frequent updates, might cause re-renders if data is updated often, which leads to performance problems.
2. **Redux:**
   - **How it Works:** A popular library with a central data store (called the store), and a strict unidirectional data flow. All data updates are dispatched using actions and reducers that update the store.
   - **Use Cases:** Complex applications with a large amount of data.
   - **Pros:** Predictable state management, easy to track changes, good for complex applications.
   - **Cons:** Boilerplate code, it is complex to learn, can be overkill for simple applications.
3. **Zustand:**
   - **How it Works:** A simple and flexible library based on hooks, which provides a centralized store.
   - **Use Cases:** Medium-sized applications. Easier to learn and use than Redux.
   - **Pros:** Simple API, easy to use, minimal boilerplate, good performance, good for medium-sized applications, and has good TypeScript support.
   - **Cons:** Not ideal for extremely large applications that have highly complex state.
4. **Recoil:**

- o **How it Works:** An atomic state management library that treats state as independent atoms, and then components can subscribe to atoms.
- o **Use Cases:** Large and complex applications, and good when you have data that is not related.
- o **Pros:** Flexible and granular state management, good performance for complex data, easy to learn.
- o **Cons:** Not very mature and has a large API, and it might be harder to debug.

5. **MobX:**
   - o **How it Works:** Allows for observable state, using classes and decorators.
   - o **Use Cases:** Applications where state changes and interactions are highly dynamic.
   - o **Pros:** Good for complex application, with a straightforward structure, and good performance.
   - o **Cons:** Class based approach, can be less common in React applications.

Practical Implementation: Using Zustand

Let's see a practical example of how to use Zustand, as it is often a good option for enterprise applications due to its simplicity.

1. Install Zustand:

```
npm install zustand
```

2. Create a store in src/store/userStore.ts:

```
import { create } from 'zustand';

interface UserState {
  isLoggedIn: boolean;
  username: string | null;
  login: (username: string) => void;
  logout: () => void;
}
```

```
const useUserStore = create<UserState>((set) => ({
    isLoggedIn: false,
  username: null,
    login: (username: string) => set(() => ({ isLoggedIn:
true, username })),
    logout: () => set(() => ({ isLoggedIn: false, username:
null })),
}));

export default useUserStore;
```

In this example, we have created a useUserStore that manages the login state for the application.

3. Use the store in a component in src/app/components/UserProfile.tsx:

```
'use client';
import useUserStore from '@/src/store/userStore';

const UserProfile = () => {
  const { isLoggedIn, username, login, logout } =
useUserStore();

  return (
    <div>
      {isLoggedIn ? (
        <div>
          <p>Welcome, {username}!</p>
          <button onClick={logout}>Logout</button>
        </div>
      ) : (
        <button onClick={() => login('John
Doe')}>Login</button>
      )}
    </div>
  );
};
```

```
export default UserProfile;
```

In this example, we are accessing the login status, the username, and the login and logout methods that are exposed by the useUserStore.

With this example, you are able to manage your application state using Zustand. You can use this approach for other components and functionalities.

Key Considerations

- **Context for Simple Cases:** Use Context API for small to medium applications, and for global settings like themes, and settings.
- **Redux for Complex Scenarios:** Use Redux for large, complex applications that require a predictable flow of data.
- **Zustand for Medium-Sized Apps:** Use Zustand for medium sized applications, because it is easy to use, and doesn't add much overhead.
- **Recoil for Granular Control:** Use Recoil when you need highly granular state management, and if you are comfortable with a new library.
- **MobX for Dynamic Applications:** Use MobX when your application is very dynamic, and you require reactivity.
- **Testability:** Make sure your state management solution supports tests.
- **Performance:** Consider the performance implications of each state management approach.

Personal Insight

I've worked on projects where the state management solution was not chosen wisely. This can lead to performance problems, code duplication, and headaches. I always emphasize that the correct state management solution is dependent on your needs, the size of your application, and your team's expertise. It is very important to have a strategy and a well thought out decision before choosing a solution.

Summary

Managing the state of an enterprise application is not simple, but if you choose the right approach, you can build a more maintainable and robust system. By carefully evaluating different state management solutions, you will be able to pick the correct one for your specific needs.

In the next section, we will discuss Authentication and Authorization strategies.

4.6 AUTHENTICATION AND AUTHORIZATION STRATEGIES

In the realm of enterprise application development, security is a top priority, and implementing robust authentication and authorization mechanisms is crucial. It's not just about building features; it's also about protecting sensitive data and ensuring only authorized users access your application. Authentication and authorization are the gatekeepers of your application, and it is very important to create a robust system.

In this section, we'll delve into the key concepts of authentication and authorization, discuss different strategies, and provide practical examples of how to implement these strategies in your Next.js 15 applications. Think of this as building a secure fortress around your application, with the right mechanisms to allow authorized users to enter and prevent unauthorized access.

Understanding Authentication and Authorization

Before we dive into specific techniques, let's clarify the core concepts:

- **Authentication:** This is the process of verifying the identity of a user. It answers the question, "Who is this user?". For example, logging into an application with a username and password.
- **Authorization:** This is the process of determining what actions a user is allowed to perform. It answers the question, "What is this user allowed to do?". For example, only an admin can delete users.

Authentication comes first, and then authorization. A user must be authenticated before you can authorize what they can do.

Key Strategies for Authentication and Authorization

Let's explore some commonly used strategies:

1. **Session-Based Authentication:**
   - **How it Works:** After a user logs in, a session is created on the server, and a session identifier is stored in a cookie on the user's browser. Each request is then authenticated with this session id.
   - **Use Cases:** Traditional web applications, suitable for monolithic architectures.
   - **Pros:** Easy to implement, and relatively straightforward.
   - **Cons:** Not suitable for distributed systems, it does not scale very well, and has security concerns.

2. **Token-Based Authentication (JWT):**
   - **How it Works:** After a user logs in, a token is generated on the server and sent to the client. The client then sends this token with each request. Tokens can be self contained and hold information about the user and its permissions.
   - **Use Cases:** Ideal for modern web applications, APIs, and microservices architectures.
   - **Pros:** Stateless, scalable, easy to implement, and flexible.
   - **Cons:** Requires careful handling of sensitive information such as signing keys, and it can be complex if the token is too large.

3. **OAuth 2.0:**
   - **How it Works:** A standard protocol for authorizing applications to access resources on behalf of a user.
   - **Use Cases:** Ideal for third-party access to resources, social logins, etc.
   - **Pros:** Secure, flexible, standardized, widely adopted.
   - **Cons:** Can be complex to implement.

4. **Role-Based Access Control (RBAC):**
   - **How it Works:** Users are assigned roles, and roles are associated with specific permissions.
   - **Use Cases:** For applications with complex user permissions.
   - **Pros:** Simple to manage and scale.
   - **Cons:** Does not support custom permission logic.

5. **Attribute-Based Access Control (ABAC):**
   - **How it Works:** Access control based on attributes, conditions, and rules.
   - **Use Cases:** For applications that require very fine-grained control over permissions.
   - **Pros:** Highly flexible, granular control.

- o **Cons:** Complex to implement and manage.
6. **API Keys:**
   - o **How it Works:** An API key is a code used to identify an application.
   - o **Use Cases:** Securing API endpoints for third parties.
   - o **Pros:** Simple to use.
   - o **Cons:** Limited security as the key can be intercepted.

Practical Implementation: JWT Authentication and Authorization

Let's implement a basic JWT authentication and authorization system in a Next.js 15 application:

1. Install jose:

```
npm install jose
```

2. Create a middleware to protect the /dashboard route in src/middleware.ts:

```
import { NextResponse } from 'next/server';
import { jwtVerify } from 'jose';

const secret = new
TextEncoder().encode(process.env.JWT_SECRET);

export async function middleware(req: Request) {
    const { pathname } = new URL(req.url);

    const token = req.headers.get('authorization')?.split('
')[1];
    if (pathname.startsWith('/dashboard')) {
        if (!token) {
            return NextResponse.redirect(new URL('/login',
req.url))
        }
    try {
        await jwtVerify(token, secret);
    } catch (e) {
```

```
      return NextResponse.redirect(new URL('/login',
req.url))
    }
  }

    return NextResponse.next();
}


export const config = {
    matcher: [
        '/dashboard/:path*',
    ],
};
```

Here we have created a middleware that will check every request that matches the /dashboard pattern. If a valid JWT is not present, the user will be redirected to the login page. We are using the jwtVerify function to verify the token, using a shared secret key. You should store your secret keys in environment variables, and avoid checking them into source control.

3. Implement a simple login in src/app/login/page.tsx:

```
'use client';

import { useState } from 'react';
import { useRouter } from 'next/navigation';
import { jwtSign } from 'jose';

const secret = new
TextEncoder().encode(process.env.JWT_SECRET);

const LoginPage = () => {
  const [username, setUsername] = useState('');
  const [password, setPassword] = useState('');
  const router = useRouter();

  const handleSubmit = async (e: React.FormEvent) => {
```

```jsx
    e.preventDefault();

    if (username === 'john' && password === '123') {
      const token =  await jwtSign({ username }, secret);
       localStorage.setItem("token", token);
       router.push('/dashboard');
    } else {
        alert('Invalid username or password');
    }
  };


  return (
    <div>
      <h1>Login</h1>
      <form onSubmit={handleSubmit}>
        <input
          type="text"
          placeholder="Username"
          value={username}
          onChange={(e) => setUsername(e.target.value)}
        />
        <input
          type="password"
          placeholder="Password"
          value={password}
          onChange={(e) => setPassword(e.target.value)}
        />
        <button type="submit">Login</button>
      </form>
    </div>
  );
};

export default LoginPage;
```

Here we have created a login form that will create a token, if the user is valid. The token will be stored in the localStorage, and the user will be redirected to /dashboard.

This is an overly simplified example, for production you might use a different authentication flow.

This provides a basic implementation of JWT authentication and authorization, that you can build upon.

Key Considerations

- **Secure Storage:** Avoid storing sensitive information in local storage or cookies. Use secure methods like HttpOnly cookies or a secure storage service.
- **HTTPS:** Use HTTPS to protect data transmitted over the network.
- **Token Validation:** Always validate tokens on the server-side.
- **Refresh Tokens:** Implement refresh tokens for long-lived sessions to keep your user logged in without frequently asking for the credentials.
- **Principle of Least Privilege:** Always grant users the minimum set of permissions necessary.

Personal Insight

In my experience, a well thought-out security strategy is a must for any application, and it is particularly important for enterprise applications. The way you implement authentication and authorization has a huge impact on the security of your system, and a security incident can be catastrophic for your business. Always prioritize security, and consider security implications in all of your development decisions.

Summary

Implementing robust authentication and authorization strategies is a critical aspect of building secure enterprise applications. By understanding the fundamental principles and adopting appropriate techniques, you can protect your application from unauthorized access, and create a secure system that your users can trust.

In the next chapter, we'll explore data handling and API integration

CHAPTER 5: ADVANCED DATA HANDLING AND API INTEGRATION

Alright, we've laid the groundwork for building scalable and secure applications, and we have seen how to structure our applications and how to manage our application's architecture. Now, it's time to delve into the intricate world of data handling and API integration, which are essential for any enterprise application. Data is the lifeblood of applications, and knowing how to fetch it, manage it, and secure it is key for building great experiences.

In this chapter, we'll explore advanced techniques for data fetching, discuss how to integrate GraphQL APIs, work with real-time data using WebSockets, implement effective caching strategies, and connect to various data sources. We'll also cover API security best practices to ensure your application is protected. This chapter will provide you with the knowledge and tools you need to build high-performing, secure data-driven applications.

5.1 OPTIMIZED SERVER-SIDE DATA FETCHING STRATEGIES

When it comes to building high-performance web applications, data fetching plays a pivotal role. And in Next.js 15, the server is where you have the most control over how you fetch your data. Server-side data fetching is not just about getting the data; it's about doing it efficiently, and responsibly, to ensure your application is fast, SEO-friendly, and provides a smooth user experience.

In this section, we'll dive deep into the world of server-side data fetching. We'll explore strategies for optimizing your data fetches, leveraging the powerful features of Next.js 15, and making data fetching more efficient. This is about making sure that data is loaded fast, and that your application is performant.

Why Server-Side Data Fetching Optimization Matters

Before we dive into specific techniques, it is important to understand why we must focus on optimizing server side data fetching.

- **Performance:** Server-side fetching improves your initial load times, making your application faster.
- **SEO:** Search engines can easily parse server-rendered content, improving your site's SEO.
- **Security:** Data fetching on the server keeps sensitive data (like API keys) out of the client-side code, and makes your application more secure.
- **Data Handling:** Fetching data on the server gives you more flexibility in how you process the data, and how you expose it to the client.
- **Flexibility:** You can perform server side data manipulation and transformations that are impossible on the client.

In summary, optimized server-side data fetching results in faster loading times, better SEO, and a more secure application.

Key Techniques for Optimized Server-Side Data Fetching

Let's discuss some strategies for optimizing data fetching:

1. **Leveraging Next.js fetch Extensions:**
   o Next.js extends the native fetch API with a set of options that can help you improve your data fetching performance.
   o **revalidate Option:** This option allows you to specify how often the data should be re-fetched, which creates a mixture between static and dynamic content. It combines the benefits of both static site generation and server side rendering, which is a powerful technique.
   o **cache Option:** This controls how data is cached by Next.js. You can specify if the data should be cached or not, by using the options 'force-cache', or 'no-store'.
2. **Parallel Data Fetching with Promise.all:**
   o Fetch data from multiple sources concurrently using Promise.all. This reduces the total time needed to load data. If you have multiple API endpoints that need to be called at the same time, this can speed up your page load.
3. **Strategic Use of Server Components:**
   o Fetch data directly within server components, which are executed on the server. This greatly improves performance and SEO.

- o Using server components will ensure that the data fetching will occur on the server and not on the client, reducing the client's work.
4. **Data Normalization:**
   - o Transform data into a format that is easier to work with in your application. This improves performance and avoids having to reformat the data on the client.
   - o Normalization can remove unnecessary data or transform the data into the correct shape that your application needs, making your data handling more efficient.
5. **Caching:**
   - o Implement caching to reduce the number of API calls, improving performance. Use revalidate for server-side caching and libraries like React Query for client side caching.
   - o Caching is very important for performance, as it avoids making unnecessary requests and improves performance.
6. **Pagination and Limits:**
   - o When you have a large amount of data, implement pagination and limits to avoid fetching more data than necessary, which speeds up loading times and prevents performance problems.
7. **Error Handling:**
   - o Implement error handling to handle issues when fetching data, and to notify the user when something goes wrong.

Practical Implementation:

Let's explore some practical examples.

1. **Fetching data with revalidate:**

```
export const revalidate = 60; // revalidate every 60
seconds

async function fetchProducts() {
  const res = await
fetch('https://fakestoreapi.com/products', {
    next: { revalidate: 60 }
  });
  return await res.json();
}
```

```
export default async function ProductsPage() {
  const products = await fetchProducts();
  return (
    <div>
      {products.map(product => <p
key={product.id}>{product.title}</p>)}
    </div>
  );
}
```

In the example above, we are using the revalidate option to refresh the data every 60 seconds. This is an example of how you combine the benefits of static site generation and server side rendering.

2. **Parallel Data Fetching:**

```
async function fetchData() {
  const [users, posts] = await Promise.all([

fetch('https://jsonplaceholder.typicode.com/users').then((res
) => res.json()),

fetch('https://jsonplaceholder.typicode.com/posts').then((res
) => res.json())
  ])
  return { users, posts }
}
export default async function MyPage(){
    const {users, posts} = await fetchData()

    return (
        <div>
            <h2>Users</h2>
            {users.map((user: any) => (<p
key={user.id}>{user.name}</p>))}
            <h2>Posts</h2>
            {posts.map((post: any) => (<p
key={post.id}>{post.title}</p>))}
```

```
        </div>
    )
}
```

In this example, we are using Promise.all to concurrently fetch users and posts, speeding up loading times.

3. **Data Normalization:**

```
    async function fetchProducts() {
  const res = await
fetch('https://fakestoreapi.com/products');
  const data = await res.json();
  return data.map((product: any) => ({
     id: product.id,
   name: product.title,
   description: product.description,
   price: product.price,
   category: product.category
  }));
}
export default async function ProductsPage() {
  const products = await fetchProducts();
  return (
    <div>
        {products.map(product => <p
key={product.id}>{product.name}</p>)}
    </div>
  );
}
```

In this example, we are normalizing the data by extracting and keeping only the fields we need, and also we are transforming them into a specific shape.

These are just a few examples of how to implement optimized server-side data fetching techniques.

Best Practices

- **Start with Server Components:** Use server components by default, and then client components as needed.
- **Cache Strategically:** Use caching for static and frequently used content.
- **Normalize Data:** Normalizing your data improves maintainability and improves performance.
- **Error Handling:** Implement proper error handling to catch API errors.
- **Monitor:** Monitor API performance and optimize data fetching as needed.

Personal Insights

From my experiences, I've seen the huge impact that data fetching strategies have on the overall performance and user experience. It's crucial to be very thoughtful about how you fetch data, and always try to optimize data fetching as much as possible. Always strive to fetch only what you need, avoid fetching data on the client whenever possible, and have a good caching strategy. I also find that monitoring API performance is key to ensure your application is working as expected.

Summary

By leveraging the optimized server-side data fetching techniques in Next.js 15, you can create high-performing and SEO friendly applications that provide a great user experience.

In the next section, we will explore how to implement GraphQL APIs with Next.js.

5.2 IMPLEMENTING GRAPHQL APIS WITH NEXT.JS

In the ever-evolving world of API development, GraphQL has emerged as a powerful alternative to REST. While REST has served us well, GraphQL offers significant advantages, especially when dealing with complex data structures and diverse client requirements. GraphQL is a query language that provides a more efficient, flexible, and powerful way to interact with your APIs.

In this section, we'll explore what GraphQL is, how it compares to REST, and how you can implement GraphQL APIs in your Next.js 15 application. Think of GraphQL as giving your clients the ability to precisely request the data they need, without over-fetching or under-fetching, improving efficiency, and performance.

Understanding GraphQL: A Different Approach to APIs

Before we get into the specifics, let's understand the core concepts of GraphQL:

- **Schema:** GraphQL uses a schema to define the types and structure of the data that can be fetched. A schema describes what data you can query from the server.
- **Queries:** Clients send queries to request data. Queries specify exactly what data you need. This avoids over-fetching of data, improving performance.
- **Mutations:** Mutations are used to modify data on the server. They are analogous to POST, PUT, and DELETE methods in REST.
- **Resolvers:** Resolvers are functions on the server that fetch the data for a specific type. Resolvers tell your GraphQL server where to fetch data from a database, or any other source.

In contrast, REST APIs typically return a fixed set of data with a standard endpoint. GraphQL gives the client much more flexibility.

GraphQL vs. REST: Key Differences

Feature	REST	GraphQL
Data Retrieval	Returns a fixed set of data from a predefined endpoint	Returns only the data that is requested by the client
Endpoints	Uses multiple endpoints	Uses a single endpoint
Data Format	Usually JSON	JSON
Flexibility	Less flexible	More flexible, clients can request exactly what they need

Over-fetching	Can lead to over-fetching	Prevents over-fetching
Under-fetching	Can lead to under-fetching	Prevents under-fetching
Schema	No schema	Uses a strong schema to define data types

Why Use GraphQL with Next.js 15?

- **Efficient Data Fetching:** GraphQL allows for efficient data fetching with precise queries, reducing over-fetching of data.
- **Performance:** GraphQL only returns the fields that are requested, this reduces the payload size, improving performance.
- **Type Safety:** GraphQL enforces strong types, which helps to find errors during development.
- **Developer Experience:** GraphQL makes it easier to work with complex APIs, as the schema acts as a clear source of truth.
- **Flexibility:** You have more flexibility to request what you need from the server, improving adaptability.

In short, GraphQL provides a more efficient and flexible way to build and consume APIs, especially in complex applications.

Implementing GraphQL in a Next.js 15 Project

Let's walk through implementing a GraphQL API in a Next.js project.

1. **Install Dependencies:** You'll need some libraries to work with GraphQL. Let's install graphql and graphql-request

```
npm install graphql graphql-request
```

2. **Set up the GraphQL Client:** Create a client to make API calls to your GraphQL endpoint. In src/lib/graphql.ts:

```
import { GraphQLClient, gql } from 'graphql-request';
```

```
  const client = new
GraphQLClient('https://countries.trevorblades.com/'); //
replace with your endpoint


  export const graphQLRequest = async (query: string,
variables?: any) => {
    const data =  await client.request(query, variables)
    return data
  }


  export const GET_COUNTRIES = gql`
      query GetCountries {
        countries {
          code
            name
        }
        }
  `;
```

Here we are creating a client to make requests to a GraphQL API. We
are also creating a query for retrieving the code and the name of all
countries. You would replace this URL with your GraphQL endpoint.

3. **Fetch Data with GraphQL:** Create a page component to use this
   client. In src/app/countries/page.tsx:

```
    import { graphQLRequest, GET_COUNTRIES } from
"@/src/lib/graphql";


export default async function CountriesPage() {
    const { countries } = await
graphQLRequest(GET_COUNTRIES)
    return (
      <div>
        <h1>Countries</h1>
          <ul>
            {countries.map((country: any) => (
              <li key={country.code}>
```

```
                    {country.name}
                </li>
            ))}
        </ul>
    </div>
)
}
```

In this example, we are fetching a list of countries using the graphQLRequest function and the GET_COUNTRIES query that we have defined in the graphql.ts file.

4. **Creating Mutations:** Let's see how you can implement a mutation. First, let's create a mutation to change the name of a continent in src/lib/graphql.ts:

```
export const MUTATE_CONTINENT = gql`
    mutation UpdateContinent($code: ID!, $name: String!)
{
        updateContinent(code: $code, name: $name) {
          code
         name
        }
      }
```

Now let's implement a page to use this mutation in src/app/continents/page.tsx:

```
'use client'
import { useState } from "react";
import { graphQLRequest, MUTATE_CONTINENT } from
"@/src/lib/graphql";

export default function ContinentsPage() {
    const [continent, setContinent] = useState({code:
"AF", name: ""})
```

```
        const [updatedContinent, setUpdatedContinent] =
useState(null)


        const handleUpdateContinent = async () => {
            const data = await
graphQLRequest(MUTATE_CONTINENT, {code: continent.code, name:
continent.name})
            setUpdatedContinent(data)
        }
        return (
          <div>
              <h2>Update Continent</h2>
              <input type="text" value={continent.code}
onChange={(e) => setContinent({...continent, code:
e.target.value}) } placeholder={"Code"}/>
              <input type="text" value={continent.name}
onChange={(e) => setContinent({...continent, name:
e.target.value})} placeholder={"New Name"} />
              <button
onClick={handleUpdateContinent}>Update</button>
              {updatedContinent &&
               <div>
               <h3>Updated Continent</h3>
               <p>Code:
{updatedContinent.updateContinent.code}</p>
               <p>Name:
{updatedContinent.updateContinent.name}</p>
               </div>
               }
           </div>
        )
    }
```

In this example, we are creating a form that sends a mutation to the
API to change the continent name.

Key Considerations

- **Choosing a GraphQL Server:** You'll need to set up a GraphQL server. There are multiple options such as Apollo Server, and GraphQL Yoga.
- **Schema Design:** Carefully design your schema so that it accurately reflects the data structure.
- **Error Handling:** Implement robust error handling for API responses.
- **Authentication and Authorization:** You must implement authentication and authorization for your GraphQL API.
- **Client-Side Caching:** Consider using libraries like Apollo Client or URQL to implement caching.

Personal Insight

In my experience, GraphQL is a great approach for modern APIs, especially when you need more control over the data that is being returned by the server. The ability to fetch exactly what you need is a game changer. It provides more flexibility than REST. While it requires an extra step, setting up your API to use GraphQL might improve your overall user experience.

Summary

By implementing GraphQL APIs in your Next.js 15 applications, you will achieve faster loading times, enhanced developer experience, and a more flexible data fetching layer.

In the next section, we will explore how to use WebSockets for real-time data handling.

5.3 REAL-TIME DATA HANDLING USING WEBSOCKETS

In the world of web development, there are scenarios where the traditional request-response model simply isn't enough. Think about a live chat application, a collaborative document editor, or a real-time stock ticker – these applications require data updates to be pushed to the client as soon as they occur. This is where WebSockets come into play. WebSockets provide a persistent, bidirectional communication channel between the client and server, allowing for real-time data exchange.

In this section, we'll explore what WebSockets are, why they are essential for real-time applications, and how to implement them in your Next.js 15 project. Think of WebSockets as a direct, always-open line of communication between your client and server, that eliminates the need to ask for new information, it just pushes it whenever something happens.

Understanding WebSockets: Real-Time Communication

Before we jump into implementation, let's understand the key concepts of WebSockets:

- **Persistent Connection:** Unlike HTTP, which is a request-response protocol, WebSockets establish a persistent connection between the client and the server. This connection remains open, and data can be exchanged in both directions.
- **Bidirectional Communication:** Data can be pushed from the server to the client (and vice-versa) without the need for a new request, allowing for efficient real-time data exchange.
- **Low Latency:** WebSockets are designed for low-latency communication, enabling real-time updates.
- **Full-Duplex:** Communication can occur simultaneously in both directions, making it perfect for interactive applications.

In contrast, HTTP requests and polling require constant requests from the client to see if there are any updates. This increases the load on the server and it's less efficient. WebSockets address these inefficiencies by establishing a connection, that stays open, and allows communication to occur immediately.

Why Use WebSockets in Enterprise Applications?

- **Real-time Updates:** Perfect for applications that require real-time updates, such as live dashboards, stock trading platforms, collaborative tools, chat applications, etc.
- **Reduced Latency:** The continuous connection offers better latency and responsiveness when compared to traditional HTTP.
- **Efficiency:** Reduces server load, since the data is sent to the client when it is available, without the need of many requests from the client.
- **Improved User Experience:** Real time updates create an engaging user experience, and provide a more interactive environment.

In short, WebSockets are essential when you need real time capabilities in your application.

Implementing WebSockets in a Next.js 15 Project

Let's implement a basic real-time chat application using WebSockets with socket.io:

1. **Install Dependencies:** You'll need socket.io for the server side and socket.io-client for the client side.

   ```
   npm install socket.io socket.io-client
   ```

2. **Create a WebSocket Server:** In your Next.js application, create an API endpoint that manages the WebSocket connection, in src/app/api/socket/route.ts:

   ```typescript
   import { Server } from 'socket.io';
   import { NextRequest, NextResponse } from 'next/server';

   const SocketHandler = async (req: NextRequest, res: NextResponse) => {
       if (res.socket?.server?.io) {
           console.log('Socket is already running');
           return res
       }

       const io = new Server(res.socket?.server);

       io.on('connection', socket => {
           console.log('New connection', socket.id);
           socket.on('chat message', msg => {
               io.emit('chat message', msg);
           });
       });
   });
   res.socket!.server.io = io;
       return NextResponse.json({msg: "ok"});
   };
   ```

```
export  {SocketHandler as GET}
```

Here we are creating a socket.io server that listens for new connections, and when it receives a chat message event, it will emit that same message to all the clients.

3. **Create a WebSocket Client:** Create a client component that will connect to your websocket. In src/app/components/Chat.tsx:

```
'use client';
import { useState, useEffect, useRef } from 'react';
  import { io } from 'socket.io-client';

  const Chat = () => {
    const [messages, setMessages] = useState<string[]>([]);
    const [newMessage, setNewMessage] = useState('');
     const socket = useRef(null)

   useEffect(() => {
     socket.current = io();

    socket.current.on('chat message', (msg: string) => {
         setMessages((prev) => [...prev, msg]);
     });

     return () => {
        socket.current?.disconnect();
      }
   }, []);

   const sendMessage = () => {
      socket.current?.emit('chat message', newMessage);
     setNewMessage('');
    };
```

```
    return (
      <div>
      <div>
          {messages.map((msg, index) => (
              <p key={index}>{msg}</p>
          ))}
      </div>
      <input
          type="text"
          value={newMessage}
        onChange={(e) => setNewMessage(e.target.value)}
      />
      <button onClick={sendMessage}>Send</button>
      </div>
    );
  };
  export default Chat
```

Here we are setting up a socket connection to the server. We listen for a chat message event, and when it happens we add the message to the list of messages. We also have a button that sends a chat message to the server.

4. **Use the Client Component:** Create a page that will use the Chat component in src/app/chat/page.tsx:

```
import Chat from "./components/Chat";

export default function ChatPage(){
  return(
      <Chat/>
  )
}
```

With this example, you have a basic chat application with real time features.

Key Considerations When Using WebSockets

- **Scalability:** WebSocket connections can be demanding. You'll need to design your server architecture to handle multiple connections.
- **Error Handling:** Implement proper error handling to handle disconnections and errors.
- **Authentication:** Authenticate WebSocket connections to ensure only authorized users can access data.
- **Security:** Protect against security vulnerabilities by sanitizing data and validating input.
- **Fallback Mechanisms:** If WebSockets are not supported, consider falling back to other techniques such as HTTP long-polling.

Personal Insight

From my experience, WebSockets can greatly improve user engagement and the interactivity of web applications. I find that knowing when to use WebSockets is the key. If your application needs real-time updates, you should definitely consider using websockets. It can also be difficult to maintain a system with websockets, but if you plan carefully, and test extensively, you will be able to have a successful implementation.

Summary

WebSockets are a key ingredient for creating real-time applications that are interactive and engaging. By learning how to implement WebSockets in your Next.js 15 applications, you'll be well-equipped to handle real time data requirements.

In the next section, we will discuss data normalization and caching techniques.

5.4 DATA NORMALIZATION AND CACHING TECHNIQUES

In the world of web development, data is often retrieved from various sources, and is returned in different formats, with different nesting levels, and with different data types. Furthermore, data is often not static, and it may be changing continuously. This is where data normalization and caching come into play, as these two techniques are a cornerstone of building efficient and performant applications, and are essential to handle the complexities of enterprise applications.

In this section, we'll explore what data normalization and caching are, why they are essential, and how to implement them effectively in your Next.js 15 applications. Think of data normalization as organizing your messy closet, and caching as storing frequently used items nearby, allowing you to access them quickly.

Understanding Data Normalization

Data normalization is the process of organizing data into a structured, standardized format. It's about making your data consistent, easy to manage, and more efficient to use. It often includes the following steps:

- **Removing Redundancy:** Eliminating unnecessary duplication of data. For example, the API might be returning too much information, so you can normalize it by removing unnecessary fields, which will improve performance.
- **Structuring Data:** Organizing data into a consistent format. Your application will become much easier to maintain if your data follows the same structure across all different endpoints.
- **Flattening Nested Structures:** Removing nested structures to make it easier to access data using simple keys.
- **Type Conversions:** Converting data into the correct data type that your application needs.

Data normalization helps to structure the data to meet the needs of your application, making the overall system more maintainable and efficient.

Why is Data Normalization Important?

- **Improved Performance:** By reducing the amount of data that needs to be transferred between client and server, you improve loading times.
- **Data Consistency:** A consistent structure makes data easier to manage and use throughout the application.
- **Reduced Complexity:** A well-normalized data structure simplifies code and reduces complexity, and makes it easier to work with.
- **Reduced Errors:** Consistent and normalized data helps to reduce errors due to type mismatches and data inconsistencies.

- **Improved Developer Experience:** Well-structured data is much easier to use and understand, improving overall development experience.

Practical Implementation: Data Normalization

Let's see a practical example. Imagine your API returns a list of products like this:

```json
[
  {
    "id": 1,
    "title": "Product 1",
    "description": "This is product 1",
    "price": {
      "amount": 10.99,
      "currency": "USD"
    },
    "category": {
      "id": "100",
      "name": "Electronics"
    }
  },
  {
    "id": 2,
    "title": "Product 2",
    "description": "This is product 2",
    "price": {
      "amount": 20.99,
      "currency": "EUR"
    },
    "category": {
      "id": "100",
      "name": "Books"
    }
  }
]
```

content_copy download

Use code with caution.Json

You can normalize it like this:

```
    async function fetchProducts() {
  const res = await
fetch('https://api.example.com/products');
  const data = await res.json();
  return data.map((product: any) => ({
     id: product.id,
     name: product.title,
     description: product.description,
     price: product.price.amount,
     currency: product.price.currency,
   categoryId: product.category.id,
     categoryName: product.category.name,
  }));
}
```

With this code, you are transforming the data into a simpler and more consistent format that makes your application easier to use and manage. The JSON response from the server has been normalized, making it flat, with clear properties, that are easy to access.

Understanding Caching Techniques

Caching is the process of storing frequently used data in a temporary storage location (cache), so that it can be quickly retrieved in the future. Caching reduces the need to fetch data from the original source, improving performance.

- **Server-Side Caching:** Caching data on the server reduces the load on the API server and improves response time.
  - o Next.js built-in caching using the fetch api.
  - o Using libraries such as Redis.
- **Client-Side Caching:** Caching data on the client's browser avoids making unnecessary API calls.
  - o Using libraries like React Query or SWR.

131

o   Browser cache.

Why is Caching Important?

- **Improved Performance:** Reduces load times by reusing data.
- **Reduced API Load:** Reduces the number of requests to the API, improving scalability.
- **Offline Support:** Allows the application to function even when the network connection is slow or unavailable (if the data has been cached).
- **Better User Experience:** Provides a smoother experience as the application responds quickly to user requests.
- **Cost Savings:** Reduces bandwidth usage and server costs.

Practical Implementation: Caching with Next.js

Next.js comes with a great caching mechanism built into the fetch API:

1. Use the revalidate option:

```
export const revalidate = 60;
```

```
async function fetchPosts() {
  const res = await
fetch('https://jsonplaceholder.typicode.com/posts', {
    next: { revalidate: 60 },
  });
  return await res.json();
}
```

In this example, the data will be revalidated after 60 seconds, providing a great balance between dynamic content and caching. This is an example of server-side caching.

2. Use React Query for client-side caching:

```
'use client';

import { useQuery } from 'react-query';
```

```
    async function fetchUsers() {
        const res = await
fetch('https://jsonplaceholder.typicode.com/users');
        return res.json();
    }


    const UsersList = () => {
        const { data, isLoading, error } = useQuery('users',
fetchUsers);

    if (isLoading) {
      return <p>Loading...</p>;
    }
    if (error) {
        return <p>Error: {error.message}</p>;
    }

    return(
      <div>
        {data.map(user => <p key={user.id}>{user.name}</p>)}
      </div>
    )
    }

export default UsersList
```

Here, we are using React Query to cache the data. The data will be cached until the cache is stale. React Query will also handle background refetches to ensure that your application is always updated.

Key Considerations for Normalization and Caching

- **Choose the right approach:** Both techniques are useful, but you must choose the right one based on your specific needs.

- **Keep it consistent:** If you decide to normalize data, do it in a consistent way, and always normalize data with the same rules, for different endpoints.
- **Cache Strategically:** Use caching wisely. Don't cache data that changes frequently.
- **Invalidate Cache:** Plan how to invalidate the cache when data is updated. React Query is a great library to handle cache invalidation.

Personal Insight

From my experience, implementing data normalization and caching makes a huge difference in how your application works. I've worked on projects where we were not normalizing or caching data, and the impact in performance was terrible. By applying these techniques, you will provide a better experience to your users. It is crucial to establish the correct strategy before building the application, as it's difficult to add these features later.

Summary

Data normalization and caching are essential for building performant, scalable, and user friendly applications. By adopting these strategies, you will have applications that have a better performance, a better experience, and are easier to maintain.

In the next section, we'll explore how to connect to various databases and data sources

5.5 CONNECTING TO VARIOUS DATABASES AND DATA SOURCES

In the world of enterprise applications, data is often spread across different databases, APIs, and other data sources. Connecting to these diverse sources and managing them effectively is a fundamental requirement for any robust application. It's not enough to just fetch data from a single database; you need to be able to seamlessly integrate with multiple sources, whether they are SQL databases, NoSQL databases, or third-party APIs.

In this section, we'll explore the challenges of connecting to diverse data sources, different strategies for doing so, and how to implement these connections effectively in your Next.js 15 application. Think of this section as building a universal adapter that allows your application to talk to any data source it needs.

The Challenge of Connecting to Diverse Data Sources

Before we jump into implementation, let's understand why connecting to different data sources is challenging:

- **Different Data Formats:** Each database and API might have its own data format, making it difficult to handle consistently.
- **Different Query Languages:** SQL databases use SQL, whereas NoSQL databases use a different approach, such as MongoDB Query Language.
- **API Variations:** Different APIs might have different endpoints, authentication methods, and response structures.
- **Complexity:** Managing multiple data sources and their connections can become complex, especially when it grows over time.
- **Performance:** Connecting to multiple data sources can impact performance if not handled correctly.
- **Security:** Securely managing credentials and access to different data sources is crucial.

In short, integrating with diverse data sources presents many challenges, but it is essential for building enterprise applications.

Strategies for Connecting to Various Data Sources

Let's explore some of the most common approaches to connect to different data sources:

1. **Object-Relational Mapping (ORM) Libraries:**
   o **How They Work:** ORMs such as Prisma and Drizzle abstract away the database interactions by providing a consistent way to manage your database schema and interact with your database.
   o **Use Cases:** Ideal for SQL databases (PostgreSQL, MySQL, SQL Server).
   o **Benefits:** Simplifies database interactions, provides type safety, provides code generation, and it can work with different databases.
   o **Drawbacks:** Can be more complex to set up than interacting directly with your database.

2. **Direct Database Connections:**
   - **How They Work:** Use a client library to directly connect to your database.
   - **Use Cases:** For SQL databases or NoSQL databases (e.g. MongoDB).
   - **Benefits:** Direct control over your database queries, good for complex queries, and more control of the performance.
   - **Drawbacks:** Less type safety than using an ORM, more manual work, and more complex when dealing with migrations.
3. **REST API Integrations:**
   - **How They Work:** Make HTTP requests to fetch data from a REST API.
   - **Use Cases:** Ideal for third-party services or microservices.
   - **Benefits:** Access to vast external resources.
   - **Drawbacks:** Can be inconsistent, and might have complex authentication.
4. **GraphQL API Integrations:**
   - **How They Work:** Make GraphQL queries and mutations to fetch and modify data.
   - **Use Cases:** Ideal for applications that require specific data, with a precise data shape.
   - **Benefits:** More efficient data fetching and more control over what is being returned.
   - **Drawbacks:** Requires a GraphQL server.
5. **Serverless Functions:**
   - **How They Work:** Use serverless functions such as AWS Lambda to connect to data sources and create API endpoints.
   - **Use Cases:** Ideal for small background processes, and data transformations.
   - **Benefits:** Highly scalable, and easy to deploy.
   - **Drawbacks:** Can be complex to maintain and debug.

Practical Implementation: Connecting to PostgreSQL using Prisma

Let's illustrate connecting to a PostgreSQL database using Prisma in a Next.js 15 application.

1. **Install Prisma CLI and Client:**

```
npm install prisma @prisma/client --save-dev
```

2. **Initialize Prisma:**

```
npx prisma init --datasource-provider postgresql
```

This command creates a prisma directory with a schema.prisma file. In this file you specify your database connection string, and your data schema.

3. **Configure your database connection:** Update the .env file with your database connection string:

```
DATABASE_URL="postgresql://user:password@host:5432/database?schema=public"
```

4. **Define your Prisma schema** in prisma/schema.prisma:

```
generator client {
  provider = "prisma-client-js"
}

datasource db {
  provider = "postgresql"
  url      = env("DATABASE_URL")
}

model User {
  id        Int      @id @default(autoincrement())
  name      String
  email     String   @unique
  posts     Post[]
}
model Post {
  id        Int @id @default(autoincrement())
  title     String
  content   String?
  authorId  Int
```

```
    author    User @relation(fields: [authorId], references:
[id])
}
```

In this example we have defined a simple User model and a Post model that have a relation with each other.

5. **Generate Prisma Client:**

```
npx prisma generate
```

6. **Push the schema to the database**:

```
npx prisma db push
```

This command creates the tables in your database.

7. **Use Prisma in your application**. In src/lib/prisma.ts:

```
    import { PrismaClient } from '@prisma/client'
const prismaClientSingleton = () => {
  return new PrismaClient()
}

type PrismaClientSingleton = ReturnType<typeof
prismaClientSingleton>
const globalForPrisma = globalThis as unknown as {
  prisma: PrismaClientSingleton | undefined
}

const prisma = globalForPrisma.prisma ??
prismaClientSingleton()

if (process.env.NODE_ENV !== 'production')
globalForPrisma.prisma = prisma
export default prisma
```

Here we are creating a singleton instance of the Prisma client that we can import in our application.

8. Create a page that uses Prisma to fetch data in src/app/users/page.tsx:

```tsx
import prisma from "@/src/lib/prisma";

export default async function UsersPage(){
    const users = await prisma.user.findMany({include:
{posts: true}})
  return(
      <div>
        <h1>Users</h1>
          {users.map(user => (
            <div key={user.id}>
                <p>Name: {user.name}</p>
              <p>Email: {user.email}</p>
               <h3>Posts</h3>
               {user.posts.map(post => (
                 <p key={post.id}>{post.title}</p>
                 ))}
            </div>
          ))}
      </div>
  )
}
```

In this example, we are fetching all the users, and their posts. This is a basic example, but demonstrates how to set up Prisma with Next.js.

Key Considerations

- **Authentication and Authorization:** Properly authenticate and authorize access to your data sources.
- **Connection Pooling:** Connection pooling improves performance by reusing database connections.

- **Error Handling:** Implement error handling to catch database errors, API errors, and other potential issues.
- **Security:** Use secure methods for storing database credentials and API keys.
- **Data Transformation:** Transform the data to the format you need.

Personal Insight

From my experiences, I've seen that it's quite common for enterprise applications to rely on data from multiple sources. Having a solid strategy on how to connect to these data sources is paramount. Using ORMs like Prisma can help reduce boilerplate, and make it easier to connect to SQL databases. Understanding how to integrate external APIs is also crucial, as this provides access to a vast amount of resources. Having a good strategy on how to fetch, normalize, and cache this data, is the key to a successful application.

Summary

Connecting to different databases and data sources is a reality for most enterprise applications, which is why it is so important to have a strategy to handle these complexities. By adopting the approaches shown here, you will have a system in place that allows you to connect to any kind of data source.

In the next section, we will explore API security best practices.

5.6 API SECURITY BEST PRACTICES (RATE LIMITING, ETC.)

In the world of web development, APIs are the backbone of modern applications, connecting clients to servers and enabling data exchange. But with great power comes great responsibility – and that means securing your APIs. APIs are often the primary target of attacks, because they expose your application's underlying resources and functionalities. Protecting your APIs is not optional, it is a critical part of building any application, especially in enterprise settings, where data is often sensitive.

In this section, we'll explore essential API security best practices, focusing on techniques like rate limiting, input validation, authentication, and more. Think of this section as building a secure perimeter around your API, protecting it from unauthorized access and malicious attacks.

Why API Security Is So Crucial

Before we jump into the specifics, let's understand why API security is critical:

- **Data Protection:** APIs often handle sensitive data. Protecting this data from unauthorized access is crucial.
- **Prevents Attacks:** A well-secured API is less prone to attacks such as SQL injections, cross site scripting, and denial of service.
- **Maintains Trust:** Protecting your API shows that you value the privacy and security of your users data.
- **Business Continuity:** API security is necessary for maintaining business continuity. A security incident can lead to disruption and loss of revenue.
- **Compliance:** Many compliance standards require strict API security measures.
- **Brand Protection:** Security incidents can impact your brand reputation.

In summary, API security is a must. It is not an option, but rather it is a requirement for any secure application.

Essential API Security Best Practices

Let's explore some key practices for securing your APIs:

1. **Rate Limiting:**
   - **How It Works:** Limits the number of requests a user or IP address can make within a specific time period.
   - **Why It's Important:** Prevents denial-of-service (DoS) attacks, and protects your infrastructure from being overwhelmed.
   - **Implementation:** You can use libraries or middleware such as express-rate-limit for Node.js, or similar solutions for other frameworks. You can also use rate limiting options provided by your hosting provider, such as Vercel or Cloudflare.
2. **Input Validation:**
   - **How It Works:** Validate all data received from the client (e.g., checking that email address is a valid format).
   - **Why It's Important:** Prevents SQL injections, cross site scripting (XSS), and other common attacks.

- o **Implementation:** Sanitize all the data that you receive from the client using libraries such as validator.js.
3. **Authentication and Authorization:**
   - o **How It Works:** Authenticate users before allowing them to access the API, and authorize actions based on their roles and permissions.
   - o **Why It's Important:** It is crucial for ensuring that only authorized users can access and modify your data.
   - o **Implementation:** Implement JWT authentication and authorization. Use OAuth 2.0 for third party access. Implement RBAC or ABAC depending on the complexity of your application.
4. **API Keys:**
   - o **How It Works:** API keys can provide access to API endpoints.
   - o **Why It's Important:** It's important to use a secure way of generating, storing, and using your API keys, as compromised API keys might lead to a breach of your system.
   - o **Implementation:** Hash, encrypt, and secure API keys.
5. **CORS (Cross-Origin Resource Sharing):**
   - o **How It Works:** Configures which domains are allowed to access your API.
   - o **Why It's Important:** Prevents unauthorized access from other domains.
   - o **Implementation:** Use your framework's or server's capabilities to set CORS headers.
6. **HTTPS:**
   - o **How It Works:** All API communication must be encrypted using HTTPS.
   - o **Why It's Important:** Protects sensitive data from being intercepted in transit.
   - o **Implementation:** Use a valid certificate and configure your server for HTTPS.
7. **Secure Storage:**
   - o **How It Works:** Use secure storage mechanisms to store API keys, and other sensitive information.
   - o **Why It's Important:** Prevents sensitive data from being exposed.
   - o **Implementation:** Use environment variables for development environments, and use a secret manager for production environments.
8. **Regular Updates:**

- o **How It Works:** Keep your frameworks, libraries, and dependencies updated, as older versions might have security vulnerabilities.
- o **Why It's Important:** It is important to always be up-to-date with all of the latest security patches.

Practical Implementation: Rate Limiting in Next.js

Let's see an example of implementing rate limiting in Next.js 15. We are going to implement the logic to limit requests for a single IP address. For more complex use cases you should consider using a dedicated service such as Redis.

1. Create a file src/lib/rateLimiter.ts:

```
const rateLimitCache = new Map<string, number>();
const REQUEST_LIMIT = 5;
const TIME_WINDOW = 60 * 1000 //60 seconds


export function checkRateLimit(ip: string) {
   const now = Date.now();
    if(rateLimitCache.has(ip)){
        const lastRequestTime = rateLimitCache.get(ip)!;
        const requests = lastRequestTime > (now - TIME_WINDOW)
? rateLimitCache.get(ip) + 1 : 1
        rateLimitCache.set(ip, requests);

        if(requests > REQUEST_LIMIT) {
        return false;
    }
      return true;
   } else {
      rateLimitCache.set(ip, 1);
      return true
   }


}
```

In this example, we are creating a map to store how many requests a certain IP has done within a specific window of time. We are using REQUEST_LIMIT to define how many requests are allowed, and TIME_WINDOW to define the period in milliseconds that will check how many requests are done.

2. Let's use this function in our /api/hello endpoint by creating src/app/api/hello/route.ts:

```
import { checkRateLimit } from '@/src/lib/rateLimiter';
import { NextResponse } from 'next/server';

export async function GET(req: Request) {
   const ip = req.headers.get('x-forwarded-for') ||
'127.0.0.1'

   const allowed = checkRateLimit(ip)

  if(!allowed){
      return NextResponse.json({message: "Rate limit
exceeded"}, {status: 429})
   }

    return NextResponse.json({ message: 'Hello from my API'
})
}
```

In this example, we get the IP address from the headers of the request, and then call our checkRateLimit function. If the function returns false, then we return a 429 status, and stop processing.

With this simple example, you can protect your APIs from abuse.

Personal Insights

From my experience, I've learned that API security is not something you implement once and forget about. It requires a continuous effort, regular audits, and constant vigilance. Always use a security-first approach when building and developing your API endpoints, and remember that one single vulnerability might lead to a disaster. Be proactive in implementing security best practices from the beginning of your projects.

Summary

Securing your API endpoints is essential for protecting your data, maintaining user trust, and ensuring business continuity. By implementing these security best practices, you'll be able to create APIs that are resilient and protected.

In the next chapter, we will discuss deployment and operations.

CHAPTER 6: PERFORMANCE OPTIMIZATION AND BEST PRACTICES

Alright, we've covered a lot of ground, from architectures to data handling, but now let's focus on something that truly separates a good application from a great one: performance. A fast and responsive application is not only crucial for user experience but also impacts SEO, and overall satisfaction of your users. This chapter is all about ensuring that the applications you build are fast, efficient, and provide a seamless experience for your users.

In this chapter, we'll delve into performance optimization techniques, best practices, and how to use the tools available to identify and fix performance bottlenecks in your Next.js 15 application. This chapter will guide you in building apps that are both functional and fast, using the tools and knowledge you already have.

6.1 CODE SPLITTING AND LAZY LOADING TECHNIQUES

When you're building a large and complex web application, the sheer volume of JavaScript code can quickly become a performance bottleneck. Users shouldn't have to download the entire application's code just to view the home page. This is where code splitting and lazy loading techniques come into play. They are essential tools for optimizing the initial load time of your application, ensuring a smoother and more engaging user experience.

In this section, we'll explore what code splitting and lazy loading are, why they're so important for web performance, and how you can implement them effectively in your Next.js 15 application. Think of these techniques as carefully organizing the ingredients for a meal—only fetching what's needed when it's needed, and ensuring everything is ready just in time.

Understanding Code Splitting

Code splitting is the process of breaking down your application's code into smaller chunks or bundles. This means that the browser only downloads the code that is required for a specific page or feature. This is different from a traditional setup where the browser downloads one large bundle, that contains everything needed for the entire application.

- **How it works:** Instead of loading all your JavaScript code in one go, you separate it into smaller bundles. When a user visits a specific page, only the code necessary for that page is downloaded, and the other code is downloaded when it is needed.
- **Types of Code Splitting:**
  - ○ **Route-Based Splitting:** Splitting code based on your application's routes.
  - ○ **Component-Based Splitting:** Splitting code based on the components that are being used on a page.

Understanding Lazy Loading

Lazy loading is a technique to load components or modules only when they are needed. For example, if you have a component that is only shown when the user clicks a button, you can lazily load the component, and avoid downloading it when the page first loads. Lazy loading is closely related to code splitting.

- **How it Works:** Instead of loading a component or module immediately, you postpone loading it until it's actually required.
- **When to Use:** Ideal for large components, modals, or offscreen content.

Why Are Code Splitting and Lazy Loading Important?

- **Faster Initial Load Times:** Users do not have to wait for the entire application to load. Only the necessary code is loaded at first, and the rest is loaded when it is needed.
- **Improved Performance:** Code splitting and lazy loading reduces the size of your application, making it more responsive.
- **Reduced Bandwidth Consumption:** Only downloading code when it is needed, improves your bandwidth consumption.
- **Better User Experience:** Creates a much more enjoyable user experience because your users do not have to wait for everything to load before being able to interact with your application.
- **Improved SEO:** Faster loading times benefit your SEO rankings.
- **Scalability:** Makes your application more scalable by reducing the initial load of your application, which helps you handle more users.

In summary, code splitting and lazy loading are crucial for building performant and scalable web applications.

Practical Implementation in Next.js 15

Next.js offers several built-in mechanisms to implement code splitting and lazy loading:

1. **Automatic Code Splitting:** Next.js automatically code splits your application by route. Each page is treated as a separate bundle and is only loaded when the user navigates to that page. This is done automatically.
2. **Dynamic Imports with import():** Use dynamic imports to load modules on demand:

```
import { useState } from 'react';

function MyComponent () {
    return <h1>Hello from my dynamic component</h1>
}

const DynamicComponent = () => {
    const [showComponent, setShowComponent] = useState(false)
     const loadComponent = async () => {
       const Component = (await
import("./components/MyComponent")).default
          return <Component/>
     }


     return (
         <div>
             <button onClick={() =>
setShowComponent(true)}>Show Component</button>
             {showComponent &&  loadComponent()}
         </div>
     )
}
```

```
export default DynamicComponent
```

In this example, the MyComponent is only imported when it is needed, and not initially when the page loads. By doing this, you do not download the code for that component unless the user clicks the button. This pattern can be used with modals or other components that are not shown by default.

3. **Lazy Loading Components with next/dynamic:** Use next/dynamic to load components lazily.
   - First, create a component src/app/components/LazyComponent.tsx:

```
function LazyComponent () {
  return <h1>Hello from lazy loaded component</h1>
}
export default LazyComponent
```

   - Now, in your page use next/dynamic:

```
import dynamic from 'next/dynamic';
const LazyComponent = dynamic(() =>
import('./components/LazyComponent'),{
    ssr: false,
    loading: () => <p>Loading...</p>
});


export default function MyPage () {
    return (
      <div>
        <h1>My Page</h1>
        <LazyComponent/>
      </div>
    )
}
```

In this example, we use next/dynamic to load a component lazily, this ensures that we do not load this code unless the component is needed.

Key Considerations

- **Loading States:** Always provide loading states when lazy loading components, or modules, to provide feedback to the user.
- **Network Performance:** Consider the network performance when loading components.
- **Test:** Test that the code is working correctly after implementing lazy loading or code splitting.
- **Avoid over-splitting:** Do not over-split code in areas that do not require it.

Personal Insight

From personal experience, I have found that code splitting and lazy loading have a huge impact on the performance of web applications. It's essential to be mindful of these techniques during the development process, and not wait until the end to implement them. By planning your code and implementing code splitting and lazy loading, you will deliver an application that is fast and enjoyable to use.

Summary

Code splitting and lazy loading are essential tools for improving the performance of your Next.js 15 applications. By implementing these techniques, you will create more performant applications that provide a much better user experience.

In the next section, we will explore how to optimize your images, and how to implement responsive design.

6.2 IMAGE OPTIMIZATION AND RESPONSIVE DESIGN

Images are a cornerstone of most web applications, and when not handled properly, they can become a major source of performance problems. Large unoptimized images can slow down page loading times, consume excessive bandwidth, and negatively impact the user experience. Optimizing images and implementing responsive design is not an optional task, it is a requirement to create performant and user friendly applications.

In this section, we'll explore the essential techniques for optimizing your images and implementing responsive design principles in Next.js 15. Think of this section as learning to become an expert in handling images, making them look great, and loading fast on any device.

Understanding Image Optimization

Image optimization involves several techniques aimed at reducing the file size of images without compromising visual quality. The goal is to provide a fast and smooth loading experience.

- **Image Compression:** Using algorithms to reduce the file size of an image by removing unnecessary data.
- **Proper Image Format:** Choosing the correct image format based on its purpose. For example, JPEG is good for photographs, while PNG is good for graphics. WebP is a newer format, and offers better compression.
- **Image Resizing:** Serving images in the correct size. Using very large images when they are being shown in smaller sizes is unnecessary, and it has a huge impact on your loading times.
- **Lazy Loading:** Loading images only when they are visible to the user.
- **Using a CDN:** Content Delivery Networks (CDNs) store your assets across the world, serving the content closer to your users, improving loading times.

Understanding Responsive Design

Responsive design is a technique to make your application adapt to different devices, and screen sizes. It is key to ensure that your images and overall design look good on mobile devices, tablets, and desktops.

- **Fluid Grids:** Designing layouts that adapt to the screen size.
- **Flexible Images:** Making your images resize based on the size of the device.
- **Media Queries:** Using CSS media queries to apply different styles based on the screen size.

Why Are Image Optimization and Responsive Design Important?

- **Faster Load Times:** Optimized images reduce the time it takes for a page to load, improving user experience.
- **Better User Experience:** A responsive design ensures that your application is easy to use on all devices, improving accessibility and usability.
- **SEO Benefits:** Search engines prioritize websites that load quickly and are mobile-friendly.
- **Bandwidth Savings:** Optimized images save bandwidth, which is a benefit for both you and the user.
- **Improved Conversion Rates:** Faster websites lead to happier users, and they are more likely to purchase a product.

Practical Implementation in Next.js 15

Let's explore some techniques for implementing image optimization and responsive design in your Next.js applications.

1. **Using next/image for Image Optimization:**

   Next.js provides a great built-in component for handling images called next/image. This component is optimized for the web and it supports lazy loading, resizing, and format conversion.

```
import Image from 'next/image';
import myImage from './my-image.jpg'; // Import your image
<Image src={myImage} alt="My image" width={500}
height={300}/>
```

   In this example, we are using the Image component to load the image, and we are also defining the width and the height of the image. Next.js will automatically generate different versions of the image, optimized for different devices. Next.js handles images by creating several optimized versions, using the WebP format when supported by the user's browser.

2. **Responsive Images with sizes:** You can use the sizes property to create more responsive images.

```
import Image from 'next/image';
```

```
import myImage from './my-image.jpg';
<Image
    src={myImage}
    alt="My image"
    width={500}
    height={300}
    sizes="(max-width: 768px) 100vw, 500px"
/>
```

In this example, we use the sizes prop, and when the screen is smaller than 768px the image will take 100vw (100% of the viewport), otherwise the image will have a width of 500px.

3. **Responsive Images with CSS:** Let's create a CSS rule that makes the image adapt to different container sizes. Create a css class, and add it to your image.

```
.responsive-image {
max-width: 100%;
height: auto;
display: block;
}
```

```
<img src="my-image.jpg" className="responsive-image"/>
```

In this example, the image will adapt to the width of the container.

4. **Lazy Loading Images:** Images are automatically lazy loaded when you use next/image. However, if you are using standard HTML <img> you can use the loading="lazy" attribute.

```
<img src="my-image.jpg" loading="lazy"/>
```

This attribute ensures that the image is loaded when it is close to the viewport.

Key Considerations

- **Use next/image:** Prefer next/image for loading images as it implements a lot of optimizations out of the box.
- **Use the right format:** Use the correct image format (WebP when supported).
- **Resize Images:** Always resize the images to the dimensions needed.
- **Compress images:** Use compression tools to reduce the file size.
- **Responsive Design First:** Think of responsive design from the start of your project.
- **Use a CDN:** Consider using a CDN to distribute your images closer to your users.

Personal Insight

From my experience, optimizing images and implementing responsive design is a constant challenge, but it is essential for building successful applications. I have seen how unoptimized images can have a huge impact in the performance of an application. Be proactive, use the tools available, and test your application on multiple devices. Remember, performance is not an option, it's a necessity.

Summary

By implementing these image optimization and responsive design techniques, you'll be able to build applications that are not only visually appealing, but also fast and accessible to all users.

In the next section, we will explore more techniques to reduce your Javascript bundle size.

6.3 ADVANCED TECHNIQUES FOR MINIMIZING BUNDLE SIZE

In the quest for building performant web applications, minimizing your JavaScript bundle size is a crucial step. A large JavaScript bundle directly impacts page load times and overall user experience. The larger the bundle, the longer it takes for the browser to download, parse, and execute your code. This results in slow loading times, and an application that is not very responsive.

In this section, we'll explore several advanced techniques you can use to keep your bundle size as small as possible, focusing on what you can do from your side, and not relying on libraries, or Next.js. Think of this as a meticulous process of pruning your codebase, removing any unnecessary code, and only using what is absolutely essential.

Why Is Minimizing Bundle Size Important?

- **Faster Load Times:** Smaller bundle sizes lead to faster initial load times, which results in a better user experience, and improve your SEO rankings.
- **Improved Performance:** Smaller bundle size reduces processing time, which improves the overall responsiveness of the application.
- **Better User Experience:** A fast and responsive application is easier to use and more enjoyable.
- **Reduced Bandwidth Usage:** Smaller bundles mean less data to download for the user. This results in reduced bandwidth usage, and is beneficial for users on slower connections.
- **SEO Benefits:** Faster loading times can result in better SEO.
- **Scalability:** Smaller bundle sizes allow your application to scale better, by reducing resource consumption.

In short, minimizing the bundle size is a key aspect of creating fast and efficient web applications.

Advanced Techniques for Minimizing Bundle Size

Let's explore several techniques you can use to reduce the bundle size of your application:

1. **Tree Shaking:**
   - **How it Works:** Removes unused code from your project. When you import a library, you might not be using the whole library. Tree shaking will remove the parts of the library that are not used.
   - **Implementation:** Modern bundlers such as Webpack or Rollup automatically support tree shaking.
   - **Best Practices:** Use ES Modules (import and export), avoid side effects, and do not import the entire library, but rather use specific imports.

```
// Instead of:
```

```
import _ from 'lodash';
_.map([1, 2], (x) => x * 2)
// Do this
 import { map } from 'lodash';
  map([1, 2], (x) => x * 2)
```

2. **Code Splitting:**
   - **How it Works:** Split your code into smaller chunks, and load those chunks lazily as needed.
   - **Implementation:** As discussed in previous sections, Next.js automatically code splits by route, and also offers the next/dynamic component for dynamically loading components.

3. **Dependency Optimization:**
   - **How It Works:** Carefully evaluate the dependencies that you are including in your project. Avoid using large libraries if you are not using all of the functionality that is provided by those libraries.
   - **Implementation:** Always look for smaller, more optimized libraries when possible.
   - **Best Practices:**
     - Avoid large dependencies.
     - Use specialized libraries instead of general purpose libraries when possible.
     - Evaluate your dependencies regularly, and remove dependencies that are not used.

4. **Compression:**
   - **How It Works:** Use compression algorithms such as Gzip or Brotli to reduce the size of your files before sending them to the user.
   - **Implementation:** Most web servers and CDNs support compression. This should be enabled in your production environments.

5. **Avoid Large Libraries:**
   - **How It Works:** Avoid using large libraries that you are only using partially. When possible try implementing the logic manually.
   - **Implementation:** Check if you are using all of the functionality of a library, if not, try implementing the feature manually if possible.

6. **Optimize Images and Assets:**
   - o **How It Works:** Optimize your images and other assets to reduce their size.
   - o **Implementation:** Use tools to compress images, and implement responsive images as shown in the previous section.
7. **Minification:**
   - o **How It Works:** Removes unnecessary characters from code (spaces, comments) without affecting the code's functionality.
   - o **Implementation:** Modern bundlers automatically support minification in production.
8. **Lazy Load Resources:**
   - o **How It Works:** Load resources such as images, videos, and components only when they are needed.
   - o **Implementation:** Implement lazy loading as discussed in the previous sections.
9. **Avoid Inline Styles:**
   - o **How It Works:** Avoid using inline styles, because they can't be cached, and they can increase the size of the HTML.
   - o **Implementation:** Use external CSS files for your styles.
10. **Use ES Modules:**
    - o **How It Works:** Use ES modules for all of your JavaScript code. This enables tree shaking.
    - o **Implementation:** Always use the import and export syntax for managing your imports and exports.

Practical Implementation: Analyzing Bundle Size

A great way to analyze your bundle size, and understand which libraries are taking up most of the space is to use the webpack-bundle-analyzer.

1. Install webpack-bundle-analyzer:

```
npm install --save-dev webpack-bundle-analyzer
```

2. Add a new script in your package.json:

```
"scripts": {
  "analyze": "ANALYZE=true npm run build"
}
```

3. Run the analysis:

```
npm run analyze
```

This command will generate a visual representation of your bundle size, which will help you find opportunities to reduce the bundle size.

Personal Insights

From my experience, constantly optimizing the bundle size is a key ingredient for building performant applications. This should be a key task for all developers in the team, and not only for the front end developers. I've seen a huge difference when the development team is aware of the impacts of bundle size, and actively look for solutions to optimize code and reduce dependency usage. A small change can lead to significant improvements.

Summary

By implementing these advanced techniques for reducing the bundle size, you will create faster applications, and you will improve the user experience, which is always a key goal in development.

In the next section, we will explore profiling techniques for your Next.js 15 applications. Do you have any questions before moving forward?

6.4 PROFILING AND IDENTIFYING PERFORMANCE BOTTLENECKS

In the journey of optimizing your web application, knowing *where* to optimize is just as important as *how* to optimize. That's where profiling comes in. Profiling is the process of measuring your application's performance, identifying performance bottlenecks, and understanding where you need to focus your optimization efforts.

In this section, we'll explore various profiling tools and techniques, with a focus on how you can identify and fix performance issues in your Next.js 15 applications. Think of profiling as becoming a performance detective, uncovering the hidden secrets of your code, and finding out why your application is slow.

Why is Profiling Important?

- **Identify Bottlenecks:** It pinpoints the areas in your application that are slowing down performance.
- **Data-Driven Optimization:** Guides your optimization efforts, so you can focus on what matters most.
- **Improved Performance:** Leads to faster load times, and a more responsive application.
- **Better User Experience:** Results in a better user experience and greater user satisfaction.
- **Scalability:** Improves scalability and reduces resource consumption.

Profiling Tools and Techniques

Let's explore some of the most useful tools and techniques for profiling your application:

1. **Browser Developer Tools:**
   o **How They Work:** Modern browsers provide built-in developer tools that allow you to analyze performance, network activity, and rendering times.
   o **Key Features:**
      - **Performance Tab:** Record application interactions and analyze performance.
      - **Network Tab:** Analyze the loading of network resources, such as images and api calls.
      - **Coverage Tab:** See which parts of your CSS and Javascript code are not used, and remove them from your code base.
   o **Practical Use:** Identify slow JavaScript functions, long network requests, and inefficient rendering practices.
2. **Next.js Profiler:**
   o **How It Works:** Next.js offers a built-in profiler that you can enable to track performance metrics. This helps you identify server side issues.
   o **How to enable:** Enable the profiler by adding ?__next_profile__ to the URL.
3. **Performance Monitoring Tools:**

- o **How They Work:** Use tools such as Sentry, Datadog, or New Relic to monitor your application's performance in production.
- o **Key Features:**
  - Real-time performance data.
  - Error tracking and reporting.
  - Alerting and monitoring.
- o **Practical Use:** Identify production issues, such as slow API calls, or problems with certain components.

4. **Webpack Bundle Analyzer:**
   - o **How It Works:** A tool that visualizes the contents of your JavaScript bundles. This will help you understand which libraries are taking up most of your bundle size.
   - o **Key Features:**
     - Visual representation of your bundle.
     - Identify large dependencies.
     - Detect code duplication.
   - o **Practical Use:** Identify large dependencies, and areas for code optimization.

5. **React Profiler:**
   - o **How It Works:** React offers its own profiler, that helps you analyze the performance of your React components.
   - o **Key Features:**
     - Identify slow rendering components.
     - Analyze the time it takes for your components to render.
   - o **Practical Use:** Identify expensive components and optimize their rendering process.

Practical Implementation: Using Browser Developer Tools

Let's explore how to use the browser's developer tools to profile your application.

1. **Open Developer Tools:** Open your browser's developer tools (usually by pressing F12 or Cmd+Option+I on a Mac).
2. **Go to the Performance Tab:** Navigate to the Performance tab, in most browsers.
3. **Start Recording:** Click the record button (usually a circular button).
4. **Interact with Your Application:** Interact with your web application, go to different pages, and click on different elements to simulate a normal user flow.

5. **Stop Recording:** Click the record button to stop the recording process.
6. **Analyze Results:** Analyze the recording:
   - **Timeline:** See the timeline, and see how long each action takes to complete.
   - **Network:** Check if you have any slow or long API calls.
   - **Main Thread:** Identify CPU bottlenecks, and long-running JavaScript functions.
   - **Rendering:** Identify slow rendering, and elements that take a long time to paint.

With this, you can identify bottlenecks and understand which part of your application is causing performance problems.

Practical Implementation: Using Next.js Profiler

1. **Enable Profiler:** Add ?__next_profile__ to your application's URL. For example http://localhost:3000/?__next_profile__.
2. **Use the Application:** Interact with your application as a normal user.
3. **Analyze the Profile:** You will see a profile in the console.
4. **Identify Issues:** Use this to find issues with your server side rendering, and data fetching.

Practical Implementation: Using Webpack Bundle Analyzer

1. Install webpack-bundle-analyzer:

```
npm install --save-dev webpack-bundle-analyzer
```

2. Add a new script to your package.json:

```
"scripts": {
"analyze": "ANALYZE=true npm run build"
}
```

3. Run the script:

```
npm run analyze
```

161

This will create a visual representation of your Javascript bundles in the browser, which will help you spot any problem with your dependencies.

Best Practices for Profiling

- **Profile Regularly:** Do not wait until the end of the project to profile your application. Profile it regularly as you develop your application.
- **Start with Real User Scenarios:** Record your profiling sessions by performing actions that a real user would perform.
- **Focus on Critical Paths:** Focus on optimizing the most critical parts of your application.
- **Use Real Devices:** If you are optimizing for mobile, profile in real mobile devices.
- **Establish Performance Baselines:** Establish performance metrics to monitor your application.
- **Iterate on Optimizations:** Make changes to your code based on your profiling, and re-profile again after each change.
- **Use Production Monitoring:** Monitor your application in the real world, by using monitoring tools such as Sentry or Datadog.

Personal Insight

From my experience, profiling is essential for identifying performance issues. It is not an option, it is a requirement. I have personally seen projects that were slow and unusable, and by using profiling tools, I have found the bottlenecks and made the necessary changes to improve performance. Always be proactive, use these tools, and make sure that your application is as performant as it can be.

Summary

Profiling and identifying performance bottlenecks is a crucial part of the development process. By understanding how to use the tools available to you, you'll be able to build faster and more responsive applications.

In the next section, we'll discuss how to leverage the built-in features of Next.js to improve your performance. Do you have any questions before moving on?

6.5 LEVERAGING NEXT.JS BUILT-IN OPTIMIZATION

Next.js is not just a framework; it's a toolkit designed to build high-performance web applications with minimal effort. A significant part of its power lies in its built-in optimization features, which can dramatically enhance your application's speed, SEO, and user experience. Understanding and leveraging these features is key to building performant applications with Next.js.

In this section, we'll explore the built-in optimization techniques that Next.js offers and how you can use them effectively to create blazing-fast applications. Think of these features as a set of powerful tools that are already provided to you, that help you optimize your application by default.

Key Built-in Optimization Features

Let's dive into the specific optimization features that Next.js provides:

1. **Automatic Code Splitting:**
   - **How it works:** Next.js automatically splits your code into separate bundles, based on your routes. Each route and component are split into their own bundle. This allows the browser to download only the code required for the current page.
   - **Why it's important:** Improves initial load times, as the user is not downloading the code for the entire application. Only the code that is needed for a specific route is downloaded at first.
   - **How to Use it:** No specific implementation is needed. Next.js handles this automatically.
   - **Best Practices:** Make sure you are using the app directory, and your components are inside the appropriate page.
2. **Image Optimization with next/image:**
   - **How It Works:** The next/image component provides a set of optimization features such as resizing images, serving them in the right format, lazy loading, and more.
   - **Why it's important:** Optimizes the way images are loaded, improving performance and user experience.
   - **How to Use it:** As shown in previous sections, always use the next/image component to load your images.
   - **Best Practices:** Always define the width, height, and alt attributes. Use responsive design techniques as shown in previous sections.
3. **Server-Side Rendering (SSR) and Static Site Generation (SSG):**

- o **How They Work:** SSR generates HTML on the server for each request, which is great for dynamic content. SSG generates static HTML pages at build time, which is great for static content.
- o **Why It's Important:** SSR improves SEO and perceived load times, and SSG is great for static content that does not change often.
- o **How to Use it:** By default, all components in the app directory are Server Components. Use server components for fetching data.
- o **Best Practices:** Use SSR for dynamic data, and SSG for static content.

4. **Incremental Static Regeneration (ISR):**
    - o **How It Works:** ISR allows you to create static pages that can be revalidated and updated in the background after a certain period of time. This mixes the benefits of both SSG and SSR.
    - o **Why It's Important:** Provides a mechanism for keeping your website updated without sacrificing performance.
    - o **How to use it:** Use the revalidate option in your fetch calls, and also set export const revalidate = 60 on a page to revalidate it every 60 seconds.
    - o **Best Practices:** Use ISR for frequently updated content, or dashboards.

5. **Built-in Support for TypeScript:**
    - o **How It Works:** Next.js has first-class support for TypeScript, which allows you to catch type-related errors early in development.
    - o **Why It's Important:** Helps reduce the number of runtime errors, which improves the overall quality of your code.
    - o **How to use it:** Create your project with TypeScript, and your application will automatically use TypeScript.
    - o **Best Practices:** Use interfaces, and types whenever you can to type your code.

6. **Fast Refresh:**
    - o **How It Works:** When you change a component, it is updated instantly in the browser.
    - o **Why It's Important:** Improves developer experience, and allows for faster development.
    - o **How to use it:** No action required. Fast Refresh is automatically configured by Next.js
    - o **Best Practices:** When debugging your code, use the fast refresh functionality.

7. **Font Optimization:**
   o **How It Works:** Next.js optimizes how fonts are loaded, ensuring that they don't slow down your initial page load time.
   o **Why It's Important:** Optimizes the way fonts are loaded, and avoids long loading times due to fonts.
   o **How to use it:** Next.js is configured by default to optimize fonts, but you should use next/font.
8. **Built-In CSS Support:**
   o **How It Works:** Next.js supports CSS Modules, Sass, and other CSS preprocessors, which helps you to better organize your styles.
   o **Why It's Important:** Allows you to create scalable and maintainable styles.
   o **How to Use it:** Configure your styles using CSS modules, Tailwind, or other technologies that are supported.
   o **Best Practices:** Avoid using inline styles. Use CSS modules, styled components, or tailwind to manage your application's styles.

Practical Implementation:

1. **SSR and SSG:**

```
export default async function MyPage(){
const data = await fetchData(); // this will fetch data
server side
  return (
    <div>
      {data.map(item => <p
key={item.id}>{item.name}</p>)}
    </div>
  )
}
```

Here, we are using SSR to fetch the data server side. If you are fetching data using client components, you are not using SSR, and you will not get the benefits of SSR.

2. **ISR with revalidate:**

```
    export const revalidate = 60 // data will revalidate
every 60 seconds.


 async function fetchData(){
    const res = await
fetch("https://fakestoreapi.com/products", {next: {
revalidate: 60 }})
     return await res.json()
 }


 export default async function MyPage(){
    const data = await fetchData()
    return (
      <div>
        {data.map(item => <p key={item.id}>{item.name}</p>)}
      </div>
    )
 }
```

Here we are using ISR, which will generate the page statically, but it will be revalidated every 60 seconds. This is a good approach when the data changes frequently.

3. **Using next/image:**

```
import Image from "next/image";
import myImage from './my-image.jpg';
 export default function MyPage(){
    return(
        <Image src={myImage} width={500} height={300}
alt="My Image"/>
    )
 }
```

Here we are using the next/image component, and Next.js will handle all the image optimization for us.

Key Considerations

- **Start Simple:** Start with Next.js defaults and gradually optimize based on your needs.
- **Monitor Performance:** Use profiling and monitoring to see how your changes are affecting the application.
- **Avoid Over-Optimization:** Do not optimize things that do not need optimization, and focus your efforts on the real bottlenecks.
- **Test:** Always test your application after making optimizations.

Personal Insight

From my experience, Next.js provides a fantastic set of tools that help you build high performance applications. You should strive to use those tools as often as you can. If you do not leverage the built in features, you will be reinventing the wheel, and will not create optimized applications.

Summary

By using the built-in features provided by Next.js 15, you'll be able to create highly optimized applications that are fast, efficient, and scalable.

In the next section, we'll explore the Core Web Vitals and how you can optimize your application based on these metrics. Do you have any questions before moving on?

6.6 UNDERSTANDING AND IMPROVING CORE WEB VITALS

In the quest for building top-notch web applications, performance is key. But it's not enough to just *feel* like your website is fast. You need to measure and understand your application's performance through a set of standardized metrics. This is where Core Web Vitals come in. They are a set of user-centric metrics defined by Google that measure the real-world user experience of your website. These metrics are key for SEO, and provide feedback on how your website is performing.

In this section, we'll explore what Core Web Vitals are, why they matter, and how you can improve your scores in your Next.js 15 applications. Think of

Core Web Vitals as a set of user experience lenses, that help you see your application through the eyes of your user.

What Are Core Web Vitals?

Core Web Vitals are a set of three metrics that focus on different aspects of the user experience. They are:

1. **Largest Contentful Paint (LCP):**
   o **What it measures:** How long it takes for the largest content element (image, video, text) to become visible on the page, from when the user requests the URL.
   o **Why it matters:** It's an indicator of how quickly a user perceives the initial content of your page to load. It is related to how quickly the user perceives the page as being useful.
   o **Good Score:** Below 2.5 seconds.
2. **First Input Delay (FID):**
   o **What it measures:** How long it takes for the browser to respond when the user interacts with a component in your page for the first time. For example, how long it takes for the browser to respond to a button click.
   o **Why it matters:** It's an indicator of how responsive your page is during initial interactions. It measures how quickly the user is able to interact with the application.
   o **Good Score:** Below 100 milliseconds.
3. **Cumulative Layout Shift (CLS):**
   o **What it measures:** How much the layout of the page shifts during loading. For example, images moving around when loading, or the text shifting as new components are added.
   o **Why it matters:** It's an indicator of visual stability. Pages that have lots of shifts are not a good experience.
   o **Good Score:** Below 0.1.

These metrics are essential because they focus on user experience, and they are also used by Google to rank search results.

Why Are Core Web Vitals Important?

- **User Experience:** Core Web Vitals directly measure real user experience, providing a user-centric approach to performance optimization.

- **SEO Ranking:** Google uses Core Web Vitals as a ranking signal in its search algorithm. Improving your scores will improve SEO.
- **Improved Conversion Rates:** Faster websites create a better user experience, which means a higher conversion rate for your application.
- **Bandwidth Usage:** Optimized applications consume less bandwidth, which leads to lower infrastructure costs, and provides a better experience for users with slow connections.
- **Better Accessibility:** Improving the CLS will also create a better experience for users that are visually impaired.

In summary, Core Web Vitals are not just about having a fast website; it's about creating a great user experience and ensuring your application is well optimized for all users.

Strategies for Improving Core Web Vitals in Next.js 15

Let's explore how you can optimize your application to improve your core web vital scores:

1. **Optimizing Largest Contentful Paint (LCP):**
   o **Optimize Images:** Use the correct image formats (WebP), compress your images, use next/image, and implement lazy loading.
   o **Optimize Text:** Reduce the amount of text on the page. Use optimized font formats.
   o **Optimize Server Response Times:** Optimize data fetching, and your API endpoints to improve response time.
   o **Prefetch Resources:** Use next/link to prefetch resources.
   o **Use a CDN:** Use a CDN to deliver assets faster.
2. **Optimizing First Input Delay (FID):**
   o **Reduce JavaScript Execution Time:** Minimize JavaScript code, reduce the amount of code that is executed on the initial load, use code splitting, and lazy load components.
   o **Defer Non-Critical JavaScript:** Load Javascript code lazily, use dynamic imports, and next/dynamic.
   o **Optimize Third Party Scripts:** Evaluate your third party scripts, and see if you can load them later, or remove them.
3. **Optimizing Cumulative Layout Shift (CLS):**
   o **Set Image Dimensions:** Always specify width and height for your images, and avoid using images without pre defined dimensions.

o **Reserve Space for Ads:** Reserve space for your ads before they are loaded, to prevent the content from shifting when the ads are loaded.
o **Avoid Inserting Content:** Avoid adding new content to your page after it has been loaded.
o **Use Transforms Instead of Layout Changes:** Use CSS transforms for animations instead of layout changes.

Practical Implementation

Let's explore how you can improve the CLS metric.

1. **Setting image dimensions**:
   o Always set the width and height properties for your images. If using next/image this is a must, and will prevent layout shifts.

```
import Image from "next/image";
import myImage from './my-image.jpg';
export default function MyPage(){
    return (
        <Image src={myImage} width={500} height={300} alt="My Image"/>
    )
}
```

2. **Avoid inserting content**:
   o Avoid inserting content dynamically on your page. This might shift your content and lead to a higher CLS. Always reserve space for elements before you load them. For example, when showing an ad, make sure to add a container with a predefined size.

Key Considerations

- **Focus on Real User Experience:** Optimize for real-world user conditions. Do not test in a perfect environment, with fast networks, etc.
- **Prioritize Key Metrics:** Focus on improving LCP and FID first, as they are usually the biggest problems.

- **Test in Multiple Devices:** Test on different devices, and screen sizes. Make sure your application is optimized for all of them.
- **Use Real Data:** Test with realistic data sets.
- **Monitor:** Monitor your Core Web Vitals using tools such as Google PageSpeed Insights, and make changes as needed.

Personal Insight

From my experience, focusing on Core Web Vitals has a huge impact in the user experience of your application. It is not enough to build something fast, it is also important to make sure that your application is responsive, that it loads properly, and that it provides a great user experience. Always optimize your application based on the needs of your users, and focus on what they perceive when interacting with

PART 3: DEPLOYMENT, OPERATIONS, AND BEYOND

CHAPTER 7: DEPLOYING YOUR ENTERPRISE APPLICATIONS

Alright, we've reached a crucial milestone in our journey – deployment! You've meticulously crafted your Next.js 15 application, optimized for performance, and now it's time to make it available to the world. Deployment is about taking your application from a local environment to a production setting, making it accessible for your users, and ensuring it is scalable, and reliable.

In this chapter, we'll explore the different deployment options available for enterprise applications, discuss how to choose the right deployment strategy, and delve into the details of zero-downtime deployments and CI/CD pipelines. This chapter will be your guide to launching your application successfully, and managing the deployment process.

7.1 DEPLOYMENT OPTIONS: CLOUD PLATFORMS AND CONTAINERIZATION

When you're ready to launch your application to the world, one of the first decisions you'll face is where and how to host it. The options available are quite broad, each with its own strengths and weaknesses. Choosing the right deployment option is not just about getting your code online; it's about ensuring your application is scalable, reliable, and secure. It's also about choosing the right option based on your team's skills, and budget.

In this section, we'll explore the two primary deployment options available today: Cloud Platforms and Containerization. We'll discuss what they are, how they work, the benefits and drawbacks, and which scenarios each option is most suitable for. Think of this section as choosing the ideal home for your application, a place where it can thrive and serve your users efficiently.

Understanding Cloud Platforms

Cloud platforms provide a managed environment for hosting your applications. They handle all the underlying infrastructure, including servers, networking, and storage. This frees you from managing the complexities of running your own infrastructure. Cloud platforms provide a variety of services, depending on your needs and your budget.

- **How They Work:** Cloud platforms provide a managed environment for your applications. You upload your application and the cloud provider handles the rest.
- **Deployment:** Deployment is as simple as connecting your repository or uploading your code.
- **Infrastructure:** Infrastructure is managed by the cloud provider, and you don't have to manage the servers directly.
- **Scaling:** Most cloud providers support horizontal and vertical scaling based on your needs.

Benefits of Using Cloud Platforms:

- **Ease of Deployment:** Cloud platforms provide a simplified deployment experience, abstracting the complexity of server configuration.
- **Scalability:** Cloud platforms offer automatic scaling, handling traffic fluctuations without any manual intervention, making your application ready for scaling at any moment.
- **High Availability:** Cloud providers offer high availability guarantees, ensuring that your application is always available.
- **Reduced Operational Overhead:** You don't have to manage any infrastructure, allowing you to focus on the code, and not on infrastructure management.
- **Cost Efficiency:** You usually pay for what you use.
- **Flexibility:** Cloud platforms offer many options depending on your needs.

Drawbacks of Using Cloud Platforms:

- **Vendor Lock-In:** You depend on a specific cloud provider, which might make it harder to migrate to another platform.
- **Cost:** Pricing can vary significantly, and can become expensive if not managed properly.
- **Limited Control:** You have less control over the infrastructure, as the infrastructure is managed by the provider.

Examples of Cloud Platforms

- **Vercel:** A popular choice for Next.js applications, offering optimized deployments, great performance, and serverless functions.
- **Netlify:** A cloud platform that offers easy deployment for static sites and single page applications.
- **AWS (Amazon Web Services):** A versatile cloud provider with a wide range of services, that can scale to meet the needs of any application.
- **Azure (Microsoft Azure):** A similar cloud provider to AWS, and is well integrated with the Microsoft ecosystem.
- **Google Cloud Platform (GCP):** A powerful cloud platform that offers many options, and great integration with the Google ecosystem.

Understanding Containerization

Containerization involves packaging your application and its dependencies into a portable container. This container can then be deployed in different environments, ensuring that your application runs consistently. Docker is the most popular technology for creating and managing containers.

- **How It Works:** You create a Dockerfile that specifies the base image, the dependencies of your application, and the configuration. You can then create an image from that Dockerfile, and that image can be deployed anywhere that Docker is supported.
- **Deployment:** You deploy the container image to your hosting environment.
- **Infrastructure:** You need to manage the infrastructure and the servers where your containers are running.
- **Scaling:** You need to manage horizontal scaling of your containers.

Benefits of Using Containerization:

- **Portability:** Containers can be deployed in any environment that supports Docker.
- **Consistency:** Containers ensure that your application works in the same way across different environments.
- **Resource Efficiency:** Containers are very efficient, as they share the resources from the host, and they are lightweight.
- **Microservices Support:** Containers are the best approach when working with microservices, as each microservice can be deployed in a separate container.

- **Customization:** You have complete control over the configuration of the container.
- **Version Control:** You can use a container registry to store different versions of your container.

Drawbacks of Using Containerization:

- **Increased Complexity:** Containerization is more complex to set up and manage than using cloud platforms.
- **Operational Overhead:** You need to manage the container orchestration and infrastructure.
- **Requires Expertise:** Requires more technical expertise.
- **Security Concerns:** You need to make sure the container is secured, and you are running the correct version.
- **Management of Resources:** You need to manage resources such as CPU, RAM, Storage for your container.

Practical Implementation:

Let's explore an example of creating a simple Dockerfile for a Next.js application:

```
# Use the official Node.js image as a base
FROM node:18-alpine

# Set the working directory in the container
WORKDIR /app

# Copy package.json and package-lock.json
COPY package*.json ./

# Install dependencies
RUN npm ci

# Copy the rest of the application
COPY . .

# Build the application
RUN npm run build
```

```
# Expose the port that the application runs in
EXPOSE 3000


# Start the application
CMD ["npm", "start"]
```

With this Dockerfile you are:

1. Using node:18-alpine as a base. This means you will be using an optimized image with node.
2. Setting the workdir for your application to /app.
3. Copying package.json, and package-lock.json.
4. Installing dependencies with npm ci.
5. Copying the rest of your application files.
6. Building your Next.js application with npm run build.
7. Exposing the port 3000.
8. Running npm start to start your application.

You can now build this image using the docker build . -t my-nextjs-app command, and run it with the docker run -p 3000:3000 my-nextjs-app command.

Choosing the Right Option

- **Startups:** For simple projects, startups, or small teams, cloud platforms are usually the best option due to ease of use, cost effectiveness, and low maintenance.
- **Enterprise Applications:** For complex enterprise applications, where more control is needed and you need a fine tuned setup, and where the organization already has the expertise, containerization is a good choice.
- **Small Teams:** If your team does not have much experience with DevOps, you should probably use a cloud platform.
- **Large Teams:** If your team has expertise with managing and creating containers, you should consider using containers.
- **Simple Projects:** If your project has very simple requirements, and you do not need to customize your server infrastructure, cloud platforms are the way to go.

- **Complex Projects:** If your project is large, and complex, and you need more control over your resources, you should consider using Docker.

Personal Insights

From my experience, I've seen that cloud platforms have completely changed the way applications are developed, and deployed. I would recommend most teams to use a cloud platform, because it greatly reduces operational complexity, allowing them to focus on creating new features. I find that Docker is an excellent option when you need total control over the runtime environment, but it requires more maintenance.

Summary

Choosing the right deployment option, either a cloud platform or containerization, is a critical decision that will affect the performance, scalability, and maintainability of your application. Be sure to evaluate your needs, your expertise, and your budget, to make the right choice for your team, and for your application.

In the next section, we'll discuss deployment strategies such as blue/green and canary deployments.

7.2 CHOOSING THE RIGHT DEPLOYMENT STRATEGY

Once you've decided *where* to host your application, the next crucial step is determining *how* to deploy it. Your deployment strategy is the process you use to release new versions of your application to your users. It's not just about pushing code; it's also about minimizing downtime, reducing risk, and ensuring a smooth user experience.

In this section, we'll explore the different deployment strategies available today. We'll discuss their advantages, disadvantages, and which scenarios they're best suited for. Think of this section as choosing the right roadmap for delivering your application, ensuring a smooth ride for your users and a stress-free process for your team.

Understanding Deployment Strategies

A deployment strategy is a plan for how you'll release new versions of your application. There are several techniques you can use depending on your needs.

- **Simple Deployments:** Deploy all the changes at once to the production environment.
- **Blue/Green Deployments:** Use two identical environments, one for the current version and one for the new version.
- **Canary Deployments:** Deploy a new version to a subset of your users.
- **Rolling Deployments:** Roll out the new version to your users gradually.

Each strategy has its own strengths and weaknesses. Choosing the right strategy is crucial for ensuring that your application is deployed reliably and without affecting your users.

Simple Deployments: The Straightforward Approach

Simple deployments, also known as "in-place" deployments, involve deploying your code directly to the existing production environment.

- **How it works:** You deploy the new version of your application directly to the servers that are already running your current version.
- **Deployment:** Usually involves replacing the files in your server or deploying a new container.
- **Rollback:** Rollbacks involve deploying a previous version.

Pros of Simple Deployments:

- **Easy to Implement:** Simple deployments are straightforward and easy to set up.
- **Low Infrastructure Costs:** Requires less infrastructure compared to other options.
- **Fast Deployments:** It is often the fastest approach, and your changes will be available quickly.

Cons of Simple Deployments:

- **Downtime Risk:** There is a risk of downtime, if the deployment fails, which makes it unsuitable for large applications.

- **Difficult to Rollback:** If the deployment fails it might be difficult to rollback to a previous version.
- **Not suitable for Complex Systems:** If your application is complex, you should probably avoid this option, as it can be risky to deploy to all your users at once.

When to use Simple Deployments:

- Small applications, development environments, low traffic applications, or non-critical deployments.

Blue/Green Deployments: The Double-Environment Approach

Blue/Green deployments involve running two identical environments: the "blue" environment that serves the current version of your application, and the "green" environment that will host the new version.

- **How it works:** You deploy your new version to the green environment, test it, and if everything is working you switch traffic from the blue environment to the green environment, making the new version available for your users.
- **Deployment:** Deploy your code to the green environment, and switch traffic when you are ready.
- **Rollback:** If something goes wrong you just switch traffic back to the blue environment.

Pros of Blue/Green Deployments:

- **Reduced Downtime:** The switch is fast and minimizes downtime.
- **Easy Rollback:** If a problem occurs, you can easily switch back to the previous version.
- **Testing in Production:** Allows you to test your application in a production-like environment.

Cons of Blue/Green Deployments:

- **Higher Infrastructure Costs:** You need to have two separate environments, increasing your infrastructure costs.
- **More Complex Setup:** Requires more initial setup and configuration.
- **Requires Load Balancer:** To switch traffic from one environment to another, you require a load balancer.

When to use Blue/Green Deployments:

- Critical applications, where downtime needs to be minimized, complex applications, and applications with a large user base.

Canary Deployments: The Gradual Rollout

Canary deployments involve releasing new code to a small subset of users first. If everything is working as expected, you can increase the percentage of users that will receive the new version.

- **How it works:** You deploy your new version to a small group of your users, while the rest remain on the old version. You monitor your system, and if everything is working as expected, you roll out the new version to the rest of the users.
- **Deployment:** Usually involves deploying to a specific subset of your servers, and a specific subset of your users.
- **Rollback:** Easy rollback, as you can quickly remove the new version, and make your users use the previous version.

Pros of Canary Deployments:

- **Reduced Risk:** Minimizes the impact of any bugs that make it to production.
- **Testing with Real Users:** Allows you to test the new version with real users.
- **Gradual Rollout:** Gives you time to monitor the new version, and make sure that it works correctly before making it available to all your users.

Cons of Canary Deployments:

- **More Complex to Implement:** Requires more complex configurations and monitoring tools.
- **Requires Monitoring:** Needs constant monitoring to find problems with the new version.
- **Inconsistencies:** Can create inconsistencies between the users that are using different versions of the application.

When to use Canary Deployments:

- Applications with large user base, applications with critical features, and when you want to test new versions before releasing to all your users.

Rolling Deployments: Gradual Updates

Rolling deployments involve updating your application by deploying new code to a subset of servers, and continuing this until all servers have the new version.

- **How it works:** You update your application on one server at a time. Once that server is updated, you update the next server, and so on.
- **Deployment:** Involves a gradual update of all servers, one at a time.
- **Rollback:** Rollback can also be implemented by deploying the old version to the servers.

Pros of Rolling Deployments:

- **Reduced Downtime:** Users will have a minimal downtime, as they will be redirected to other servers if one server is not responding.
- **Easy Rollback:** You can easily roll back by deploying the old version to all servers.
- **Less Risky:** As only a subset of the users are using the new version at the same time, you can easily detect any problems before they affect all users.

Cons of Rolling Deployments:

- **More complex:** More complex than simple deployments.
- **Requires careful planning:** Requires careful planning to avoid issues with the upgrade process.

When to use Rolling Deployments:

- Applications with many users, large applications, and systems that need gradual updates.

Practical Implementation

While implementing these strategies from scratch can be complex, most cloud platforms such as Vercel, Netlify, and AWS provide mechanisms to implement these strategies, often without any extra configuration.

1. **Vercel:** For example, in Vercel, when you push to your main branch, the new version will be deployed to a new environment, and it will become the default version.
2. **AWS:** In AWS you can use Elastic Beanstalk to implement Blue/Green deployments, and you can also implement rolling deployments with EC2 and other AWS technologies.

Personal Insight

From my experience, I have seen that choosing the right deployment strategy is one of the most important decisions you can make. It determines the reliability and availability of your application. I always emphasize the importance of planning carefully, and choose a strategy that is based on your project and team's needs. There is no single correct answer, and you must evaluate all the options, and choose the one that best meets your requirements.

Summary

Choosing the right deployment strategy is not a technical decision only; it's also a business decision. By choosing the right strategy, you are creating a more reliable and robust application for your users.

In the next section, we'll explore how to implement zero-downtime deployments for your applications. Do you have any questions before moving on?

7.3 IMPLEMENTING ZERO-DOWNTIME DEPLOYMENT TECHNIQUES

In today's always-on digital world, users expect applications to be available at all times. Downtime, even for brief periods, can lead to user frustration, loss of revenue, and damage to your brand's reputation. This is where zero-downtime deployment techniques come into play. Zero-downtime deployments are strategies that allow you to release new versions of your application without any interruptions to the user experience, ensuring that your application is always available, and new code can be deployed reliably.

In this section, we'll explore the core concepts of zero-downtime deployments, different techniques, and how you can implement them effectively in your Next.js 15 applications. Think of zero-downtime deployments as a seamless and invisible upgrade of your application, making sure the user experience is not interrupted at any point during the update.

Why Are Zero-Downtime Deployments Important?

- **Improved User Experience:** Avoids any service interruptions and ensures that the application is always available, resulting in a better user experience.
- **Business Continuity:** Zero downtime deployments are essential for maintaining continuous operations.
- **Reduced Risk:** Minimize the impact of any bugs that are deployed to production, as you can easily roll back if something goes wrong.
- **Increased Reliability:** Helps create a more reliable deployment process, and reduces manual interventions, and human errors.
- **Faster Development Cycles:** It allows for more frequent deployments, which helps in improving development velocity.
- **Brand Reputation:** Reliable systems improve your brand's reputation, and provide confidence in your application.

In short, zero-downtime deployments are crucial for any application that needs to be always available, especially for enterprise level applications.

Techniques for Implementing Zero-Downtime Deployments

Let's explore the different techniques you can use to implement zero-downtime deployments:

1. **Blue/Green Deployments:**
   - **How it works:** As we have discussed in the previous sections, you have two identical environments, a blue environment that hosts the old version, and a green environment that hosts the new version. Once the new version is tested, you switch traffic to the new environment.
   - **Benefits:** Offers an easy and quick way to deploy new versions and minimize downtime. Rollbacks are easy by just switching back to the blue environment.
   - **Implementation:** Uses load balancers to redirect traffic to the new version of the application, usually configured in your cloud platform.
2. **Rolling Deployments:**

- o **How it works:** New code is deployed to a subset of servers, then gradually to all servers. This ensures that only a small subset of your users is impacted if there is any problem.
- o **Benefits:** Gradually updates your system without any downtime.
- o **Implementation:** Usually implemented with container orchestration systems such as Kubernetes, or in your cloud provider platform.

3. **Canary Deployments:**
   - o **How it works:** You roll out your new version to a small subset of users first. Once you are sure that everything is working as expected, you deploy it to more users.
   - o **Benefits:** Allows you to test with real users, and roll back if necessary.
   - o **Implementation:** Can be implemented with load balancers, or service mesh technologies.

4. **Load Balancers:**
   - o **How it Works:** Load Balancers distribute traffic to multiple servers, and they are a crucial component in implementing zero-downtime deployments.
   - o **Benefits:** Distribute traffic across different servers, improves scalability, and ensures that your website is always available.
   - o **Implementation:** Configure a load balancer on your cloud platform, or by using a service such as NGINX or HAProxy.

5. **Database Migrations:**
   - o **How it Works:** Manage database changes carefully. Avoid making breaking changes. Apply changes in a non-breaking way, and use strategies such as blue/green or rolling deployments for your database migrations.
   - o **Benefits:** Avoids database related downtimes when releasing a new version of the application.
   - o **Implementation:** Use tools such as Prisma Migrate, or similar technologies.

Practical Implementation: Blue/Green Deployments with Vercel

Let's see how to implement zero-downtime deployments using Vercel:

1. **Vercel Automatic Deploys:** Vercel automatically creates a new deployment every time you push a commit to your Git repository.
2. **Production Branch:** In Vercel, you can set up which branch is your production branch. Every commit that is pushed to your production

branch will be deployed to production, replacing the previous version.

3. **Preview Deployments:** Vercel creates preview deployments for every branch that is not your production branch. You can use the preview deployments to test changes before merging them to production.

4. **Automatic Domain Routing:** When you deploy a new version, Vercel automatically switches traffic to the new version.

With Vercel, you do not have to do any extra configurations. You only push code to your main branch, and Vercel handles the rest for you.

Practical Implementation: Zero Downtime Database Migrations with Prisma

Prisma is a tool that has a built-in migration system. Here are the steps you can follow to apply database migrations:

1. **Create Migration:** Make changes to your database schema in your schema.prisma file. Use npx prisma migrate dev to create a new migration. This command will generate a migration file and apply the migration locally.

2. **Apply Migrations:** In production you should use npx prisma migrate deploy to apply your migrations. This will apply the migration safely in production, and prevent any down time due to schema changes.

With this you are ensuring that your database is correctly updated when you are releasing new versions of your code, which is essential for zero downtime deployments.

Key Considerations

- **Testing:** Thoroughly test your deployments before making them available to all users.
- **Monitoring:** Monitor your applications for any issues after the deployment.
- **Rollback Strategy:** Plan for rollbacks in case something goes wrong.
- **Database Migrations:** Plan database migrations carefully, always make sure your database changes are backward compatible.
- **Load Balancers:** Use load balancers to route traffic to healthy instances.
- **Rolling Updates:** Implement rolling updates whenever possible.

Personal Insight

From my experience, implementing zero-downtime deployment is a must for large, and complex applications. I've been involved in projects where deployments caused major downtime, leading to very frustrating experiences for the user, and also for the development team. By using zero downtime strategies, we greatly improved the reliability of the applications, and we were able to deploy new versions without any interruptions.

Summary

Zero-downtime deployment is not just a technical challenge; it's a necessity for providing a seamless user experience and ensuring your application is always available. By adopting these techniques, you'll be able to provide a more reliable and resilient service, making your application better for all of your users.

In the next section, we will explore how to automate deployments with CI/CD pipelines.

7.4 AUTOMATING DEPLOYMENTS USING CI/CD PIPELINES

In today's fast-paced development world, manual deployments are not only slow, but also error-prone and tedious. To truly optimize your deployment process, you need to embrace automation. Continuous Integration and Continuous Deployment (CI/CD) pipelines provide a powerful solution for automating the build, test, and deployment phases of your application. They help you release new features and bug fixes faster, with more reliability, and they allow your team to focus on development rather than manually deploying your code.

In this section, we'll explore what CI/CD pipelines are, why they're essential, and how you can implement them effectively for your Next.js 15 applications. Think of CI/CD as an automated factory for your code, which takes your code, puts it through a series of checks, and then reliably and automatically delivers your application to the production environment.

Understanding CI/CD Pipelines

Before diving into implementation, let's understand the core concepts:

- **Continuous Integration (CI):** A practice where code changes from multiple developers are frequently merged into a shared repository. CI pipelines automatically build, test, and validate the code.
- **Continuous Deployment (CD):** A practice where code changes are automatically deployed to production after passing all the checks in the CI phase.

CI and CD work together to automate the entire software release process.

Why Are CI/CD Pipelines Essential?

- **Faster Release Cycles:** CI/CD automates the release process, allowing for more frequent and faster releases.
- **Reduced Human Error:** Automation reduces human intervention and human errors.
- **Improved Code Quality:** Automated testing helps in detecting issues before they make it to production.
- **Increased Productivity:** Automating deployment frees developers from tedious manual tasks, and allows them to focus on writing new code.
- **Faster Feedback Loops:** CI/CD provides faster feedback on changes, which speeds up the development process.
- **Consistency:** By automating the process you guarantee a consistent way of deploying new versions, with the same steps, every time.

In summary, CI/CD pipelines are crucial for automating the release process, and they are a cornerstone of modern software development.

Key Components of a CI/CD Pipeline

A typical CI/CD pipeline consists of the following stages:

1. **Source Control:** The pipeline starts when changes are pushed to your version control system (e.g., Git).
2. **Build:** The source code is compiled, and packaged into deployable artifacts.
3. **Test:** Automated tests are run to verify that the new code works correctly.
4. **Deploy:** If all tests pass, the code is deployed to a production or staging environment.

5. **Monitoring:** The application is monitored after deployment to detect any performance or stability issues.

Implementing CI/CD Pipelines for Next.js 15

Let's explore how you can implement a CI/CD pipeline using GitHub Actions and Vercel:

1. **Configure Vercel:** Connect your Git repository to Vercel. Vercel provides a very simple and straight forward way to deploy Next.js applications.
2. **Create a GitHub Actions Workflow:** Create a file in .github/workflows/main.yaml:

```yaml
name: CI/CD Pipeline


on:
  push:
    branches:
      - main


jobs:
  build:
    runs-on: ubuntu-latest
    steps:
      - uses: actions/checkout@v3
      - uses: actions/setup-node@v3
        with:
          node-version: 18
      - run: npm ci
      - run: npm run build
  deploy:
    needs: build
    runs-on: ubuntu-latest
    steps:
      - name: Deploy to Vercel
        uses: amondnet/vercel-action@v20
        with:
```

```
              vercel-token: ${{ secrets.VERCEL_TOKEN }}
              vercel-org-id: ${{ secrets.VERCEL_ORG_ID }}
              vercel-project-id: ${{
secrets.VERCEL_PROJECT_ID }}
```

Let's break this configuration down:

- o name: Defines the name of the workflow.
- o on: Defines when this workflow should run. In this example the workflow will run every time there is a commit to the main branch. You can change this to another branch if that is your deployment branch.
- o jobs: Defines the jobs that will be executed.
  - build: This job will checkout your code, set up node.js, install dependencies, and build your application.
  - deploy: This job depends on the build job. It will deploy your application to Vercel. It uses the amondnet/vercel-action action, which you must configure by setting up the required secrets for your Vercel project in Github.

With this basic workflow, every time you push changes to the main branch, your application will be automatically built, tested (you might want to add more tests in your build step), and deployed to Vercel.

Key Considerations

- **Testing:** Add unit tests, integration tests, and end-to-end tests to your pipeline. This will ensure that your application is thoroughly tested before it is deployed.
- **Environment Variables:** Always configure your environment variables, as they might be different for different environments.
- **Security:** Make sure that you are protecting your secrets and API keys, and are following security best practices.
- **Monitoring:** Always monitor your application after deployment, and set up alerts to notify you of any errors.
- **Rollbacks:** Have a strategy in place to easily roll back if there is a problem with the new deployment.
- **Deployment Strategies:** You can use a different deployment strategy than the default deployment process. For example, if you want to

deploy with a blue/green strategy, you can add more steps to your workflow.

Alternative CI/CD Tools:

While GitHub Actions is excellent for GitHub projects, here are some alternative CI/CD options:

- **GitLab CI:** A powerful CI/CD tool that is deeply integrated with GitLab.
- **Jenkins:** A self-hosted open source automation server.
- **CircleCI:** A cloud based CI/CD tool.
- **Azure DevOps:** Microsoft's DevOps solution.
- **AWS CodePipeline:** A CI/CD tool that is integrated with AWS.

Personal Insight

From my experience, having a well defined and robust CI/CD pipeline is a game changer in how applications are delivered. It completely removes the manual deployment effort, and it provides a predictable, and reliable way to release software. By spending time and resources in automating your deployments, you will reduce the time it takes to deploy new features, and you will also reduce the number of errors that will make it to production.

Summary

By implementing CI/CD pipelines, you'll be able to automate your deployments, improve code quality, and speed up the release process. This will create a better development experience for your team, and will improve the reliability of your software.

In the next chapter, we will explore strategies for monitoring, logging, and managing errors.

CHAPTER 8: MONITORING, LOGGING, AND ERROR MANAGEMENT

Alright, we've deployed our application and it's now available to users. But the journey doesn't end there. In fact, it's just beginning. Now it's time to think about how we're going to ensure that our application continues to perform well, detect errors, and provide the best user experience possible. That's where monitoring, logging, and robust error handling become absolutely crucial.

In this chapter, we'll explore how to set up monitoring tools, implement effective logging practices, handle errors gracefully, and debug issues that arise in production. This chapter will be your guide to maintaining your application's health and ensuring it runs smoothly for all your users. This is about keeping a close eye on your application, and proactively resolving any issues that arise.

8.1 SETTING UP MONITORING TOOLS (SENTRY, DATADOG)

In the realm of software development, particularly in the fast-paced world of web applications, it's not enough to simply build and deploy your application. You also need to be able to continuously monitor its performance, identify issues, and react promptly. This is where monitoring tools come into play. They provide a crucial window into your application's behaviour, allowing you to detect problems before they impact your users.

In this section, we'll explore how to set up two popular monitoring tools, Sentry and Datadog, for your Next.js 15 applications. Think of this section as installing a sophisticated security system for your application that not only monitors for break-ins but also provides valuable insights on your applications general health.

Why Are Monitoring Tools Important?

Before we dive into specific tools, it's important to understand why you should spend time on setting up monitoring:

- **Proactive Issue Detection:** Monitoring tools help you identify issues before they affect your users, allowing you to take action immediately.
- **Performance Insights:** You will gain visibility into your application's performance, allowing you to find bottlenecks and optimize your code.
- **Error Tracking:** It's essential for tracking errors, crashes, and exceptions that happen in production, so you can understand what is going on.
- **Improved User Experience:** By identifying and fixing issues, you create a better user experience.
- **Scalability:** With a monitoring system you can make better scaling decisions based on usage, and performance insights.
- **Data-Driven Decisions:** Monitoring provides data that helps in making better decisions about your application's future.

In short, monitoring tools are a must-have for any production application, especially in enterprise environments.

Sentry: Error Tracking and Performance Monitoring

Sentry is a powerful tool that focuses on error tracking and performance monitoring. It's great for identifying, grouping, and prioritizing errors, and understanding how your application performs.

- **Key Features:**
    - Error tracking with detailed stack traces, and user information.
    - Performance monitoring with insights into slow API requests, loading times, and slow components.
    - Integration with other tools such as Slack, and Github.
    - User tracking.

Practical Implementation: Setting up Sentry

1. **Create a Sentry Account:** Go to sentry.io and create a free account.
2. **Create a New Project:** Create a new project in Sentry. Select React or Next.js as your platform. Sentry will generate a DSN (Data Source Name), which you will need later.
3. **Install the Sentry SDK:**

```
npm install @sentry/nextjs
```

4. **Configure Sentry in next.config.js:** Update your next.config.js with the following:

```
    // next.config.js
const { withSentryConfig } = require('@sentry/nextjs');

const moduleExports = {
    // Your other Next.js configurations
};


const sentryWebpackPluginOptions = {
    // Additional config options for the Sentry Webpack
plugin.
// Suppresses source map uploading logs during builds
    silent: true,
};


module.exports = withSentryConfig(moduleExports,
sentryWebpackPluginOptions);
```

Here we are adding the withSentryConfig, which will ensure that Sentry is correctly configured when you build your application.

5. **Initialize Sentry SDK:** Create a new file called src/lib/sentry.ts:

```
import * as Sentry from '@sentry/nextjs';

 const SENTRY_DSN = process.env.NEXT_PUBLIC_SENTRY_DSN;

 Sentry.init({
    dsn: SENTRY_DSN,
    tracesSampleRate: 1.0, // Trace every transaction
});
```

Here we are importing the Sentry SDK, and initializing it using the NEXT_PUBLIC_SENTRY_DSN environment variable. We are also setting the tracesSampleRate to 1, this means that we will track all transactions.

6. **Wrap your application with Sentry:** In src/app/layout.tsx:

```
import "./globals.css";
import type { Metadata } from "next";
import Header from "./components/Header";
import Footer from "./components/Footer";
import * as Sentry from './lib/sentry';

export const metadata: Metadata = {
    title: "My Enterprise App",
    description: "The best app ever",
};

export default function RootLayout({
    children,
}: {
    children: React.ReactNode;
}) {
    return (
        <html lang="en">
          <body>
            <Sentry.ErrorBoundary fallback={<p>Something went wrong</p>}>
                <Header/>
                {children}
                <Footer />
            </Sentry.ErrorBoundary>
          </body>
        </html>
    );
}
```

Here, we wrap our whole application with the Sentry.ErrorBoundary component. This means that if an error happens in any component, Sentry will catch it. This error will then be sent to your Sentry dashboard.

7. **Set Up Environment Variables:** Add NEXT_PUBLIC_SENTRY_DSN to your .env.local file and any other environment file that you need. The value of the environment variable should be your DSN (Data Source Name) from Sentry.

Now, Sentry is set up to monitor your application.

Datadog: Monitoring and Analytics Platform

Datadog is a full-featured monitoring and analytics platform that is used in many enterprise environments. It provides a wide range of monitoring capabilities for your applications, servers, and services.

- **Key Features:**
  - Application Performance Monitoring (APM).
  - Infrastructure monitoring.
  - Log management.
  - Real user monitoring.
  - Dashboards and visualizations.

Practical Implementation: Setting up Datadog

1. **Create a Datadog Account:** Go to datadoghq.com and create a free trial account.
2. **Create a New Application:** In the Datadog UI, create a new application, and create a client token.
3. **Install the Datadog Real User Monitoring (RUM) Library:**

```
npm install @datadog/browser-rum
```

4. **Initialize the Datadog SDK:** Create a new file called src/lib/datadog.ts:

```
import { datadogRum } from '@datadog/browser-rum';

const DATADOG_APP_ID = process.env.NEXT_PUBLIC_DATADOG_APP_ID
```

```
const DATADOG_CLIENT_TOKEN =
process.env.NEXT_PUBLIC_DATADOG_CLIENT_TOKEN
const DATADOG_ENVIRONMENT =
process.env.NEXT_PUBLIC_DATADOG_ENVIRONMENT

if (DATADOG_APP_ID && DATADOG_CLIENT_TOKEN) {
  datadogRum.init({
      applicationId: DATADOG_APP_ID,
      clientToken: DATADOG_CLIENT_TOKEN,
      site: 'datadoghq.com',
      service: 'my-enterprise-app',
      env: DATADOG_ENVIRONMENT,
      // Specify a version number
      version: '1.0.0',
      sampleRate: 100,
      premiumSampleRate: 100,
      trackResources: true,
      trackLongTasks: true,
      trackUserInteractions: true,
  })
}
```

5. **Import Datadog:** Import this file in src/app/layout.tsx:

```
import "./globals.css";
import type { Metadata } from "next";
import Header from "./components/Header";
import Footer from "./components/Footer";
import './lib/datadog';

export const metadata: Metadata = {
    title: "My Enterprise App",
    description: "The best app ever",
};

export default function RootLayout({
```

```
    children,
}: {
    children: React.ReactNode;
}) {
    return (
        <html lang="en">
          <body>
            <Header/>
            {children}
            <Footer />
          </body>
        </html>
    );
}
```

6. **Set up Environment Variables:** Add the following environment variables to your .env.local, and other environment files. You will find these variables in your Datadog project settings.

```
    NEXT_PUBLIC_DATADOG_APP_ID=your-datadog-app-id
NEXT_PUBLIC_DATADOG_CLIENT_TOKEN=your-datadog-client-token
NEXT_PUBLIC_DATADOG_ENVIRONMENT=your-environment-name
```

Now, Datadog will start collecting data from your application, and you can use the Datadog UI to track performance, errors, and more.

Key Considerations

- **Choose the right tool for your project:** There are many different monitoring tools. Choose the tool that best fits your needs.
- **Configuration:** You need to spend time in properly configuring your monitoring tool, to ensure that it meets your requirements.
- **Security:** Protect your API keys, and secrets from being exposed.
- **Data Privacy:** Be aware of your data privacy policies, and avoid collecting sensitive data that you do not need.
- **Integrations:** Integrate monitoring tools with your other applications and services, to get a holistic view of your entire system.

Personal Insights

From my experience, setting up monitoring tools is a must for any production application. It is not an optional task. I recommend to set up your tools from the beginning of your project, not after you have an issue. Monitoring tools are essential to proactively address issues, and to understand how your application is performing in the real world. It is key to have visibility on how your users are using your application.

Summary

By implementing monitoring tools such as Sentry or Datadog, you'll be able to keep track of your application's health and performance, proactively identifying, and resolving issues before they affect your users.

In the next section, we'll discuss effective logging strategies.

8.2 EFFECTIVE LOGGING STRATEGIES AND PRACTICES

In the intricate world of software development, logging is a fundamental practice that plays a critical role in understanding your application's behavior, troubleshooting issues, and maintaining overall system health. Logging is not just about writing console.log statements; it's about implementing a systematic approach to recording events in your application, making them readily available for analysis.

In this section, we'll explore the importance of logging, different logging levels, how to implement effective logging strategies, and practical techniques that you can apply to your Next.js 15 application. Think of this section as building a comprehensive audit trail for your application, which will help you understand what happened, and what is happening, at any point in time.

Why Are Logging Strategies and Practices Important?

- **Troubleshooting and Debugging:** Logs are essential for tracking down errors and understanding the context of those errors.

- **Performance Analysis:** Logs can provide insights into the performance of your application. By logging how long certain processes take, you can pinpoint performance bottlenecks.
- **Security Auditing:** Logs provide an auditable record of user actions, which is crucial for security and compliance.
- **Understanding User Behavior:** Logs can help you understand how your users are interacting with your application.
- **Monitoring:** Monitoring tools often rely on log data to provide insights and alerts, which helps create a proactive system that automatically identifies issues.
- **Business Intelligence:** Logs can be used for business intelligence, to track data, and performance of different areas of your application.

In summary, well implemented logging is not optional, it is key for maintaining, debugging and understanding your application.

Key Principles of Effective Logging

Before we dive into the practical aspects, let's discuss the key principles of effective logging:

1. **Use Log Levels:** Classify your log messages by severity to make it easier to find errors, and warnings in a sea of information. The most common levels are:
   - debug: Information useful for debugging, that is generally not used in production.
   - info: General information about the operation of your application.
   - warn: Indicates potential issues that do not stop the application from functioning but should be addressed.
   - error: Records errors that happened in the application.
   - fatal: Records critical errors that stopped the application from working.
2. **Use Structured Logging:** Use a structured format such as JSON for your logs. This makes it much easier to parse, analyze, and query logs, specially if you are using log management systems.
3. **Include Context:** Include the necessary context to understand the log message. For example, the user ID, session ID, request ID, component name, or any other relevant information that can help when troubleshooting an issue.

4. **Log Appropriately:** Do not over log, but make sure you log the key aspects of your application. You should only be logging what is essential, and try to avoid logging sensitive data.
5. **Avoid Logging Sensitive Data:** Do not log passwords, API keys, or other sensitive information. Make sure to never include personally identifiable information (PII) unless it is absolutely necessary.
6. **Centralized Logging:** Send your logs to a central logging service such as Elasticsearch, Splunk, or Datadog. This makes it much easier to analyze and troubleshoot your application.
7. **Rotate Logs:** Set up a system to rotate your logs, to prevent filling up the disk space on your servers.
8. **Be Descriptive:** Write clear and concise log messages, explaining what happened, and the reason for the error or warning.

Practical Implementation in Next.js 15

Let's explore how to implement some of these principles in your Next.js 15 application.

1. **Creating a Simple Logging Function:**

```
const log = (level: string, message: string, context?:
any) => {
   const logObject = {
      level,
      message,
       timestamp: new Date().toISOString(),
      context,
   };
   console.log(JSON.stringify(logObject));
};

export default log;
```

In this example, we create a reusable logging function that can be used in our application. This function accepts a level, message, and a context as parameters. The log function will create a log object with all the details, and output it as a JSON string. This simple

201

implementation shows how you can improve your logging strategy, even with basic tools.

2. **Using the Log Function:**

```
    import log from "@/src/lib/logger";
const myFunc = () => {
  log("info", "My function was called", {userId: "user123"});
  try {
    throw new Error("Something went wrong")
  } catch (e: any) {
    log("error", e.message, {location: "myFunc"})
  }
}
```

With this approach, you can create consistent, and useful log statements in your application, while also providing the right level of context.

3. **Using a Third-Party Logging Library (Winston):**
   You can also use a third party logging library to implement your log system. Let's see how to use winston.
   o   Install Winston:

```
npm install winston
```

   o   Create a Logger Utility Function in src/lib/winston.ts:

```
import winston from 'winston';

const logger = winston.createLogger({
    level: 'info',
    format: winston.format.combine(
        winston.format.timestamp(),
      winston.format.json()
    ),
  transports: [
```

```
      new winston.transports.Console(),
   ],
});
```

4. const log = (level: string, message: string, context?: any) => {
   logger.log(level, message, { context });
   }
   export default log

5. Here we are creating a basic Winston logger that sends all logs to the
   console. You can easily configure Winston to send your logs to other
   destinations, like files, or cloud based log storage services.
   o   Use the Winston Logger in your components:

```
import log from "@/src/lib/winston";

const MyComponent = () => {
   log("info", "My component was rendered")
   return <div>Hello from My component</div>
}


export default MyComponent
```

Using a library like Winston allows you to easily customize
the output, and the way your logs are stored, offering a much
more robust solution than just using console.log.

Key Considerations

- **Choose the Right Log Levels:** Carefully choose the level for your
  logs.
- **Context Is Key:** Always include enough context in your logs, to
  make it easier to find issues.
- **Be Specific:** Make your logs descriptive and actionable.
- **Centralize Your Logs:** Send your logs to a centralized service.
- **Do Not Log Sensitive Information:** Do not log any sensitive
  information, or PII.
- **Use Structured Logging:** Always log using a structured format such
  as JSON.

Personal Insight

From my experience, I've seen how crucial effective logging is for debugging production issues. I have been involved in projects where logs were hard to read, and did not provide the context that was needed to understand the problems. I have also been involved in projects where logs were nonexistent. The key is to be consistent with your approach, and always provide enough context to ensure the logs are useful. The effort you put into logging will pay off many times over when you need to debug an issue in your application.

Summary

Effective logging is a critical skill for building and maintaining any application, especially in enterprise settings. By adopting the principles and strategies outlined here, you'll be able to create a robust logging system that provides visibility, and allows you to keep track of your application's health.

In the next section, we'll explore how to handle errors robustly in production.

8.3 HANDLING ERRORS ROBUSTLY IN PRODUCTION ENVIRONMENTS

In the real world of production environments, errors are inevitable. No matter how well you test your code, unexpected issues will arise. Handling these errors gracefully is crucial for maintaining the stability of your application, preventing crashes, and ensuring a smooth user experience. It's not just about avoiding errors; it's about planning for them, so that when they happen, your application is able to handle them efficiently.

In this section, we'll explore essential techniques for handling errors in production, focusing on how to implement these strategies in your Next.js 15 application. Think of this section as building a robust safety net for your application, so when something goes wrong, your application does not crash, and provides the best possible experience to the user.

Why Is Robust Error Handling Important?

- **Prevent Crashes:** Handles errors gracefully and prevents your application from crashing or becoming unresponsive.
- **Improved User Experience:** Provides meaningful error messages, and avoids displaying cryptic error messages to the users, improving user experience.
- **Faster Problem Resolution:** By logging errors, and using error monitoring tools you can identify and fix problems faster.
- **Application Reliability:** Proper error handling makes your application more reliable and less prone to problems.
- **Security:** Prevents attackers from exploiting uncaught errors.
- **Maintain User Trust:** By handling errors correctly, you are also protecting your users data, and you are showing that you have a reliable application.

In short, robust error handling is key for ensuring the stability, reliability, and usability of your applications.

Key Strategies for Robust Error Handling

Let's explore the strategies you can implement to catch and handle errors correctly:

1. **try...catch Blocks:**
   - **How it works:** Use try...catch blocks to handle errors that may occur during the execution of a specific code block.
   - **When to Use It:** Use them to wrap code that is likely to throw errors, such as API calls, data manipulation, database queries, or any other potentially unsafe operation.
   - **Best Practices:** Log the error message, and provide a meaningful fallback message for your users.
2. **Error Boundaries:**
   - **How It Works:** Use React Error Boundaries to catch errors that occur during rendering of a React component, or its children.
   - **When to Use It:** Use them in your root layout, or in any other component that renders many children components.
   - **Best Practices:** Always include a fallback component that informs the user that something went wrong. Use the error boundary to log the errors to a logging system, or to send them to a monitoring tool.
3. **Global Error Handlers:**

- o **How it Works:** Create a global error handler to catch errors that are not caught by try...catch blocks or error boundaries.
- o **When to Use It:** Catch uncaught exceptions that happen anywhere in your application.
- o **Best Practices:** Log the error, and provide a generic error message to your users.

4. **API Error Handling:**
   - o **How It Works:** Handle errors that happen in your API endpoints such as invalid parameters, database connection issues, or internal server errors.
   - o **When to Use It:** Always implement proper error handling in your API endpoints.
   - o **Best Practices:** Return a meaningful error response that tells the user what happened.

5. **Consistent Error Messages:**
   - o **How It Works:** Always provide meaningful and consistent error messages.
   - o **When to Use It:** In all parts of your application.
   - o **Best Practices:** Use a well-defined structure, and provide helpful error messages.

6. **Error Logging:**
   - o **How it works:** Always log errors to a logging system, and implement proper log levels.
   - o **When to Use It:** Always log errors in development, staging, and production.
   - o **Best Practices:** Include context information with the error messages, such as user ID, session ID, component name, and timestamp.

Practical Implementation in Next.js 15

Let's explore how to implement some of these techniques in your Next.js 15 application:

1. **Using try...catch Blocks:**

```
import log from "@/src/lib/logger";

const fetchData = async () => {
    try {
        const res = await fetch("https://myapi.com/data");
```

```
    if(!res.ok) {
      throw new Error("Could not fetch data")
    }
  return await res.json();
} catch (e : any) {
    log("error", e.message, {location: "fetchData"})
    return null
  }
}
```

In this example, we wrap the API call with a try...catch block, which logs the error, and returns null if there is an error.

2. **Error Boundaries:** Let's create a component that uses Sentry's error boundary:

```
import * as Sentry from '@/src/lib/sentry';

const MyComponent = () => {
  throw new Error('This is an example of an error in my
component');
    return (
      <div>My component</div>
  )
};

export default function ErrorPage() {
    return(
      <Sentry.ErrorBoundary fallback={<p>Something went
wrong</p>}>
        <MyComponent/>
      </Sentry.ErrorBoundary>
  )
}
```

In this example, we are using Sentry.ErrorBoundary to catch the error happening in MyComponent, and we are rendering a fallback message. The error will be sent to Sentry automatically.

3. **Global Error Handler:** While there is no global error handling in Next.js 15 by default, you should always handle errors on a component level, and use a component wrapper such as Sentry.ErrorBoundary to wrap your root layout, or the components that render the rest of the application.
4. **API Error Handling:** In your API endpoints, make sure to handle errors and return an appropriate response:

```
import { NextResponse } from 'next/server'
export async function GET() {
    try{
      throw new Error("Something went wrong")
    }
    catch (e: any){
       return NextResponse.json({error: e.message}, {
status: 500 });
      }
}
```

In this example, the API endpoint catches any error that happens, and returns a JSON response with the error message, and an status code of 500, which indicates an internal server error.

Key Considerations

- **Log Errors:** Always log errors that happen in your application, even if you are handling them gracefully.
- **User Feedback:** Always display a message to your users when an error happens, and let them know what happened, and what to do next.
- **Use Error Boundaries:** Always use React Error Boundaries.
- **Test your error handling:** Test error conditions to ensure that all cases are covered.

Personal Insights

From my experience, I've learned that robust error handling is not an option, it is a requirement for any production application. I have seen a lot of applications that crash, and give very little feedback to the user, or do not provide any logs. I have also been involved in projects where error handling was an afterthought, and the result was a buggy application, with a bad user experience. It is important to remember that by handling errors correctly, you are providing a much better experience for your users.

Summary

Handling errors correctly is crucial for ensuring that your applications are reliable, and provide a good experience for your users. By using try...catch blocks, error boundaries, and implementing error logging, you'll create an application that is resilient, and provide a good experience even when errors occur.

In the next section, we will explore how to debug production applications using several different techniques.

8.4 DEBUGGING TECHNIQUES FOR PRODUCTION NEXT.JS APPLICATIONS

Debugging in a production environment can feel like navigating a maze in the dark. Unlike development environments where you have access to debuggers and full control, production is a black box, with real users, real data, and a whole new set of challenges. Knowing how to debug effectively in production is an essential skill for any developer, especially when you are building enterprise applications that have high availability and reliability requirements.

In this section, we'll explore several strategies and techniques that you can use to debug issues in your production Next.js 15 applications, focusing on how to diagnose and solve problems when you don't have a traditional debugger at your fingertips. Think of this section as becoming a skilled investigator, using all the clues available to solve the mystery of why your application is not working as expected.

Why is Debugging in Production Challenging?

Before we jump into solutions, let's explore why debugging in production is complex:

- **Limited Access:** You don't have direct access to the code, and the environment is different from your local setup.
- **Real User Traffic:** Issues occur under real user load, which can be difficult to simulate locally.
- **Complex Systems:** Applications often involve multiple services and components, making it hard to pinpoint the source of a problem.
- **Time Constraints:** Issues need to be resolved quickly to avoid business disruptions.
- **Limited Visibility:** You can't just open up your browser's debugger and see what's going on.

With all of these challenges, it is important to have a robust strategy for debugging production issues.

Strategies for Debugging Production Applications

Let's explore the best techniques to help you troubleshoot issues in your production environments:

1. **Effective Logging:**
    - **How it works:** As we discussed in the previous section, using structured logging, with the correct log levels is key to understanding your applications behavior in production.
    - **Best Practices:** Use logging to track user activity, monitor key processes, track errors, API calls, database queries, and important server events.
2. **Monitoring Tools:**
    - **How they work:** Monitoring tools such as Sentry and Datadog provide visibility into your application's performance, and help you track errors.
    - **Best Practices:** Set up alerts for critical errors, and use performance dashboards to identify bottlenecks.
3. **Server-Side Logs:**
    - **How they work:** Access and review server-side logs to check for any errors that might be happening on your server.
    - **Best Practices:** Understand how your logs are being stored, rotated, and managed.
4. **Browser Developer Tools:**

- o **How they work:** While you might not have access to source code in the browser dev tools in a production environment, you can still use them to check for networking issues, browser errors, and frontend performance.
- o **Best Practices:** Use the network tab to monitor slow requests, and the performance tab to track front end performance.

5. **Analyzing Error Messages:**
   - o **How they work:** Carefully examine the error messages provided by your application or monitoring tool. Error messages often provide enough information for you to find the cause of the problem.
   - o **Best Practices:** Try to understand the error, and the context of the error to be able to diagnose the issue.

6. **Reproducing Issues:**
   - o **How they work:** Try reproducing the issue on a staging or development environment, to see the steps that trigger the problem.
   - o **Best Practices:** Use the information provided by your logging systems, to simulate the behavior. If you can reproduce the issue, you can debug it with your local tools.

7. **Feature Flags:**
   - o **How they work:** Use feature flags to control which users see the new feature, allowing you to isolate bugs and roll out fixes easily.
   - o **Best Practices:** Always use a strategy to roll out new features. Do not release the new feature to all users if it is not tested thoroughly.

8. **Remote Debugging:**
   - o **How they work:** Some cloud providers offer remote debugging tools.
   - o **Best Practices:** While not recommended in production, you can use remote debugging in staging, and development.

9. **Use Metrics:**
   - o **How they work:** Always monitor key metrics such as API response times, database query times, and any performance indicators.
   - o **Best Practices:** Use tools such as Grafana or Prometheus to monitor your application in production, and set up alerts to notify you if there is an issue.

Practical Implementation: Using Server-Side Logs

Let's see how to check server logs in Vercel:

1. **Log in to Vercel:** Login to your Vercel account.
2. **Select Your Project:** Select the project that you want to debug.
3. **Navigate to Logs:** Go to the Analytics section, and select the Logs tab.
4. **Filter:** Filter the logs by your production environment, or by the specific deployment you want to debug.
5. **Analyze:** Analyze your server side logs for any error messages, and warnings that might give you more information about the issue you are investigating.

Practical Implementation: Using Browser Developer Tools

1. **Open Developer Tools:** Open the browser developer tools by pressing F12 or Cmd+Option+I on a Mac.
2. **Navigate to the Network Tab:** Open the network tab to inspect API calls, or load times for your resources.
3. **Navigate to the Console Tab:** Check the console for any Javascript errors that might be happening.
4. **Navigate to the Performance Tab:** Use the performance tab to find if there are any bottlenecks in your front-end code.

With these tools, you can gather information about how your application is behaving in production.

Key Considerations

- **Reproduce Issues:** Whenever you can, try to reproduce the problem in a testing environment.
- **Use Logs:** Use logs to understand the problem, and the context.
- **Avoid Making Changes Directly in Production:** Always test changes in a test environment.
- **Always Be Proactive:** Do not wait for an issue to happen. Always be proactive in improving logging, monitoring, and observability of your system.

Personal Insight

From my experiences, I have found debugging in production to be one of the most difficult tasks in software engineering. However, if you have a well-defined strategy, you can effectively troubleshoot and fix the issues that might arise. The key for solving production problems is to be proactive in logging, monitoring, and to use all the tools that are available to you to gather as much information as possible.

Summary

Debugging production applications is not easy, but if you implement effective logging strategies, monitoring tools, and you have a solid methodology to troubleshoot production problems, you will be able to successfully fix any issue that might arise.

In the next chapter, we will explore essential security practices.

CHAPTER 9: SECURITY PRACTICES FOR ENTERPRISE APPLICATIONS

Security is not an optional add-on; it's a fundamental requirement for any enterprise application. In today's digital world, where data breaches are increasingly common, building secure applications is not just a best practice—it's a necessity. This is especially important in enterprise settings, where applications handle sensitive data, and are constantly exposed to different threats.

In this chapter, we'll explore the essential security practices you need to implement when developing enterprise applications. We'll discuss secure coding practices, managing sensitive data, conducting security audits, and complying with data privacy regulations. This chapter will be your guide to building applications that are not only functional but also highly secure. This is about becoming a guardian of your application's security and protecting it from any vulnerabilities.

9.1 SECURE CODING PRACTICES: PREVENTING COMMON VULNERABILITIES

In the ever-evolving landscape of web development, security vulnerabilities are like hidden landmines, waiting to be triggered by careless coding practices. While no system can ever be 100% secure, adopting secure coding practices is the most important step in preventing the majority of common vulnerabilities that attackers exploit to compromise applications. Secure coding isn't just a checklist; it's a mindset of building secure software from the ground up.

In this section, we'll explore essential secure coding practices that you should implement in your Next.js 15 applications, focusing on how to prevent common vulnerabilities. Think of this section as learning the art of building your application like a fortress, with the right strategies and techniques to keep the bad guys out.

Why Are Secure Coding Practices Important?

- **Prevents Attacks:** Secure coding helps prevent common attacks like SQL injections, cross-site scripting (XSS), and cross-site request forgery (CSRF), which can lead to data breaches and system compromises.
- **Protect User Data:** It helps protect sensitive user data such as passwords, and personal information, by making it harder for attackers to get access to it.
- **Ensures Application Reliability:** Prevents your application from being compromised and helps you create more reliable applications.
- **Reduces Costs:** Implementing secure coding early in the process is much more cost effective than fixing security vulnerabilities after the application is deployed.
- **Maintains User Trust:** Secure applications inspire user trust and confidence.
- **Reduces Liability:** Reduces the risk of fines, and legal actions related to data breaches.
- **Maintains Business Continuity:** Prevents costly service outages due to security breaches.

In short, secure coding practices are the first line of defense against all types of attacks.

Key Secure Coding Practices

Let's explore some key techniques to help you build more secure applications:

1. **Input Validation and Sanitization:**
   - **How it works:** Always validate and sanitize data that comes from the client. This means validating that the input data has the correct format, and that it is not malicious.
   - **Best Practices:**
     - Use libraries to validate common inputs such as email addresses, phone numbers, etc.
     - Sanitize HTML using libraries such as DOMPurify.
     - Always validate data on the server, do not rely only on client side validation.
2. **Output Encoding:**
   - **How it works:** When you render data that is coming from the user, make sure to properly encode the data to prevent XSS attacks.
   - **Best Practices:**

- Use React's automatic encoding mechanisms.
- Use a library like escape-html when rendering data.
- If you are rendering HTML from a server, always sanitize it.

3. **Parameterized Queries (Prepared Statements):**
   o **How it Works:** Using parameterized queries to avoid injecting SQL code in your database queries. When using parameterized queries, you are creating a SQL query, where all parameters are inserted safely, avoiding any SQL injection.
   o **Best Practices:** Always use parameterized queries when communicating with your database. Do not concatenate strings when building database queries.
   o **Implementation:** Use the built in support for parameterized queries on your database connector.

4. **Secure Authentication and Authorization:**
   o **How it Works:** Implement robust authentication and authorization mechanisms.
   o **Best Practices:**
      - Use secure password storage techniques (bcrypt, argon2).
      - Do not store secrets in code. Use environment variables, or secret managers.
      - Implement proper access controls, using roles and permissions.
      - Always validate tokens on the server side.
      - Use multi-factor authentication whenever possible.

5. **HTTPS:**
   o **How It Works:** Always use HTTPS to encrypt all communication between the browser and the server.
   o **Best Practices:** Use valid TLS certificates and configure your server to enforce HTTPS.

6. **CORS:**
   o **How it works:** Implement CORS (Cross Origin Resource Sharing) to control what domains can access your API endpoints.
   o **Best Practices:** Set the appropriate CORS headers.

7. **Security Headers:**
   o **How it works:** Use security headers to prevent certain types of attacks.
   o **Best Practices:** Add headers such as:
      - X-Frame-Options: To prevent clickjacking.
      - X-Content-Type-Options: To prevent mime sniffing.

- Referrer-Policy: To control what referrer information is sent.
- Strict-Transport-Security (HSTS): Enforce HTTPS usage.

8. **Regular Security Updates:**
   - **How it works:** Regularly update your dependencies to prevent security issues.
   - **Best Practices:** Use tools such as npm audit, or yarn audit to check for security vulnerabilities in your dependencies.

9. **Principle of Least Privilege:**
   - **How It Works:** Grant the minimum required permissions for users, and services. This reduces the impact of compromised accounts or services.
   - **Best Practices:** Only give the required access to each user.

Practical Implementation:

1. **Input Validation with Zod:**

```
import { z } from 'zod';

const schema = z.object({
  email: z.string().email(),
  password: z.string().min(8),
  name: z.string().min(2).max(50),
});

const validateInput = (input: any) => {
  try {
    schema.parse(input);
    return true
  } catch (e) {
    return false;
  }
}
```

With Zod, you can easily validate your data types, and formats.

2. **Sanitize HTML with DOMPurify:**

```
import DOMPurify from 'dompurify';

const MyComponent = ({userInput}) => {
 const sanitizedHtml = DOMPurify.sanitize(userInput)
 return <div dangerouslySetInnerHTML={{ __html:
sanitizedHtml}} />
}
```

DOMPurify will remove any potential malicious code from the HTML.

3. **Parameterized Queries with Prisma:**

```
import prisma from '@/src/lib/prisma';
const getUserByEmail = async (email: string) => {
  const user = await prisma.user.findUnique({
    where: {
    email,
   },
  });
 return user
};
```

Prisma will make sure that the data is correctly sanitized and that SQL injections are not possible.

4. **Setting Security Headers:** You can set security headers using middleware in Next.js:

```
import { NextResponse } from 'next/server';

export function middleware(req: Request) {
  const res = NextResponse.next();
    res.setHeader("X-Frame-Options", "DENY");
    res.setHeader("X-Content-Type-Options", "nosniff");
```

```
    res.setHeader("Referrer-Policy", "no-referrer");
  return res;
}
```

Here, we are setting security headers for all our responses.

Personal Insights

From my experience, I've found that secure coding should not be something that you do at the end of your project, but rather, it should be something that you do from the start, and you must always follow security best practices. By incorporating security principles early and proactively, you'll create applications that are less susceptible to attacks. Developers should always be aware of the security implications of their decisions, and always be looking for ways to improve code security.

Summary

Secure coding practices are a crucial element in your application's security. By implementing the best practices, you'll be able to greatly improve the security of your applications, and protect your user's data.

In the next section, we'll discuss how to manage sensitive data and API keys securely.

9.2 SECURELY MANAGING SENSITIVE DATA AND API KEYS

In the world of application development, particularly in enterprise settings, we often work with sensitive data, such as database credentials, API keys, user secrets, and other confidential information. Improper handling of this data is a major security risk, which can lead to data breaches, unauthorized access, and severe consequences for your application, and for your organization. The key is to always treat any sensitive data, as if it was a highly valuable treasure, and to make sure that it is protected at any cost.

In this section, we'll explore best practices for managing sensitive data and API keys securely, focusing on what to avoid, and how to protect your application, and your users. Think of this section as learning how to manage sensitive information with the utmost care, ensuring that it's always protected, and only accessible when it's absolutely necessary.

Why is Secure Management of Sensitive Data Important?

- **Data Protection:** Sensitive data needs to be protected from unauthorized access, because if compromised, your application, and your users will be vulnerable.
- **Compliance:** Many regulations (such as GDPR, CCPA, HIPAA) require organizations to protect sensitive data.
- **Prevents Breaches:** Improper handling of sensitive data can result in data breaches, which can be devastating for your business, and for your user's privacy.
- **Maintains User Trust:** Protecting user data improves user trust and maintains the integrity of your organization.
- **Avoids Financial Loss:** Data breaches can lead to significant financial losses.

Best Practices for Managing Sensitive Data and API Keys

Let's explore several techniques that you can use for managing your sensitive data:

1. **Never Store Secrets in Code:**
   o **Why it's important:** Storing secrets directly in your codebase will lead to a security issue. Secrets that are stored in your code are easily discovered if your code is compromised.
   o **Best Practices:** Always store sensitive information in environment variables, or in secure secrets management systems.
2. **Use Environment Variables for Development:**
   o **How it works:** In your local environments, you can use environment variables by setting up a .env.local file.
   o **Best Practices:** Use the .env.local file to store development settings.
3. **Use a Secrets Manager for Production:**
   o **How it Works:** Use a dedicated secrets manager provided by your cloud platform to securely store and manage your secrets.
   o **Benefits:** Centralized storage, access control, audit logs, versioning, and encryption of your secrets.

- o **Examples:** AWS Secrets Manager, Azure Key Vault, Google Cloud Secret Manager.
- o **Best Practices:** Use your cloud provider's API or SDK to retrieve your secrets, do not use the web UI to get the secrets.

4. **Implement Principle of Least Privilege:**
   - o **How it works:** Only grant the minimum level of access that is necessary for each role, user, and service.
   - o **Benefits:** Reduces the risk of security incidents, as access is restricted.
   - o **Best Practices:** Audit and update user, and service permissions regularly.

5. **Use Role-Based Access Control (RBAC):**
   - o **How It Works:** Use RBAC to assign roles to different users and services, limiting what resources they can access.
   - o **Benefits:** Helps in managing access, and provides a granular approach to managing permissions.
   - o **Best Practices:** Always grant the minimum necessary permission to every user, and service.

6. **API Key Rotation:**
   - o **How It Works:** Set up a regular rotation of your API keys. This means that your API keys should be regularly invalidated, and new keys must be created.
   - o **Benefits:** If an API key is compromised, it will only be valid for a limited period of time, which will minimize the potential damage.
   - o **Best Practices:** Automate your API key rotation using your cloud provider.

7. **Encrypt Data at Rest and in Transit:**
   - o **How It Works:** Encrypt your data when it is stored, and when it is being transferred, to protect it from unauthorized access.
   - o **Best Practices:** Use TLS/SSL to encrypt data in transit, and use a encryption algorithm to encrypt data at rest.

8. **Audit Access:**
   - o **How It Works:** Audit access to your sensitive data, and API keys.
   - o **Benefits:** Track any anomalies, and potentially detect if there has been a breach.
   - o **Best Practices:** Create an audit strategy that covers all access to your resources.

9. **Use Separate Accounts:**

- o **How It Works:** Use different accounts for development, staging, and production environments.
- o **Benefits:** Isolates different environments, and minimizes the risk of exposing production secrets.
- o **Best Practices:** Do not use your personal credentials in production. Use service accounts instead.

Practical Implementation: Using Environment Variables

1. **Create an .env.local file:**
   Create a .env.local file in your project's root directory, and add your API keys and secrets, for example:

```
NEXT_PUBLIC_API_KEY=my-api-key
DB_URL=postgres://myuser:password@localhost:5432/mydatabase
```

2. **Access Environment Variables:** You can now access the environment variables in your code by using process.env:

```
const apiKey = process.env.NEXT_PUBLIC_API_KEY
const dbUrl = process.env.DB_URL
```

   Important: Always avoid adding the .env.local file to your version control, and always make sure to use different secrets for different environments.

Practical Implementation: Using AWS Secrets Manager

1. **Create Secrets in AWS Secrets Manager:** Create your secrets in AWS secrets manager, store your API keys, database passwords, etc. You can then use the AWS Console, the CLI, or the AWS SDK to create the secrets.
2. **Retrieve Secrets in your application:** Use the AWS SDK to access your secrets:

```
import { SecretsManagerClient, GetSecretValueCommand }
from "@aws-sdk/client-secrets-manager"
const retrieveSecret = async (secretName: string) => {
```

```
const client = new SecretsManagerClient({
    region: 'your-aws-region', // set your AWS region here
});
const command = new GetSecretValueCommand({
    SecretId: secretName,
  });
    try {
      const response = await client.send(command);
      const secret = JSON.parse(response.SecretString || "")
    return secret
  } catch(error) {
      console.error("Error retrieving secret:", error);
      return null
    }
}


const getApiKey = async () => {
  const secret = await retrieveSecret("my-api-key");
   return secret.apiKey
}
```

With this example, you are fetching the secret from AWS, without hardcoding the keys in your code.

Key Considerations

- **Do not store keys in code:** Avoid storing secrets in code at any cost.
- **Use secrets managers:** Use a secrets manager for production environments.
- **Use RBAC:** Implement role-based access control to limit who can access your secrets.
- **Rotate your secrets:** Always rotate your secrets on a regular basis.
- **Encrypt your secrets:** Encrypt your secrets at rest and in transit.
- **Audit access:** Always audit who is accessing your secrets.

Personal Insights

From my experience, handling sensitive data and API keys securely is a continuous process, that should always be a top priority. I have seen projects where secrets were stored in the codebase, and were eventually compromised, leading to security issues. Always be aware of the best practices, and use them in every part of your development process.

Summary

By implementing these best practices, you will greatly improve your application's security. By using secure storage, API key rotation, and RBAC, you are putting in place the first steps to secure your application, and your user's data.

In the next section, we will discuss security audits, and penetration testing.

9.3 REGULAR SECURITY AUDITS AND PENETRATION TESTING

In the never-ending battle against cyber threats, building secure applications is just the first step. You also need to be proactive in identifying vulnerabilities, and testing your security defenses. This is where regular security audits and penetration testing come into play. These processes help you find weaknesses in your system before attackers do, allowing you to fix any security flaws before they can be exploited.

In this section, we'll explore what security audits and penetration testing are, why they are crucial for enterprise applications, and how you can implement them in your Next.js 15 projects. Think of this section as regularly inspecting your fortress for weaknesses, hiring experts to try to break in, and patching any holes that you find to make your application more secure.

Why Are Security Audits and Penetration Testing Important?

- **Proactive Security:** They help identify vulnerabilities before they can be exploited by attackers.
- **Improve Code Quality:** These practices improve the security of your code, by forcing you to focus on security concerns.
- **Compliance:** Many compliance standards require regular security audits, and penetration testing.

- **Maintains Security Posture:** It keeps your security mechanisms up-to-date with the latest techniques and attack patterns.
- **Reduces Risk:** Reduces the risk of costly security breaches and data leaks.
- **Peace of Mind:** Having a regular security audit and penetration testing strategy gives you peace of mind, by ensuring that your application is secure.

In summary, security audits and penetration testing are fundamental aspects of maintaining a strong security posture for your organization, and for your application.

Understanding Security Audits

A security audit is a systematic assessment of your application, its infrastructure, and its processes to find weaknesses, and vulnerabilities. A security audit is like a thorough medical checkup, for your application.

- **How it works:** Code is reviewed to identify security flaws, your infrastructure configuration is checked, and your security policies are evaluated.
- **Scope:** It covers everything from code quality, configuration, authentication mechanisms, and data handling practices.
- **Objective:** To identify potential security risks and areas for improvement, and also provide solutions.
- **Who performs it:** Internal security teams or external experts can perform the audit.

Key Areas of Focus in a Security Audit:

- **Code Review:** Assess code quality, and adherence to security guidelines.
- **Configuration Review:** Check the configuration of your servers, firewalls, databases, and other components.
- **Authentication and Authorization:** Review how you handle authentication and authorization.
- **Data Handling:** Review how your application handles sensitive data.
- **API Security:** Review all your API endpoints.
- **Infrastructure Security:** Review the security settings in your infrastructure.
- **Compliance:** Make sure that your application complies with industry standards and legal requirements.

- **Policies:** Review your security policies to ensure they are effective and up to date.

Practical Implementation: Performing a Code Review

1. **Gather Your Team:** Gather your team of developers that have a good understanding of the security best practices.
2. **Schedule Code Review:** Schedule a code review session for the specific modules that need to be reviewed.
3. **Review Code:** Check for vulnerabilities and insecure coding practices in the code.
4. **Make Recommendations:** Create a list of recommendations of what should be changed, or improved.
5. **Follow Up:** Follow up and make sure the code has been updated, and all recommendations have been applied.

Understanding Penetration Testing

Penetration testing is a simulated cyberattack designed to find vulnerabilities in your application by simulating real-world attack scenarios. This process involves ethical hackers using the same tools, and techniques that malicious attackers would use to find vulnerabilities in your system.

- **How It Works:** A third party attempts to exploit weaknesses in your application.
- **Scope:** Usually focuses on external facing vulnerabilities.
- **Objective:** To find security holes and report them to the development team.
- **Who performs it:** Ethical hackers or security experts perform penetration tests.

Key Areas of Focus in Penetration Testing:

- **Network Security:** Scanning your network for open ports, and services with known vulnerabilities.
- **Authentication and Authorization:** Checking for vulnerabilities in your authentication, and authorization mechanisms.
- **Input Validation:** Checking if you are sanitizing the user inputs.
- **SQL Injection:** Testing for SQL injection vulnerabilities.
- **XSS:** Checking if there are XSS vulnerabilities.
- **CSRF:** Testing if the application is protected from CSRF attacks.
- **API Security:** Testing API endpoints.

Practical Implementation: Using Static Analysis Tools

1. **Set up a Static Analysis Tool:** Install a static analysis tool such as SonarQube, or ESLint in your project.
2. **Configure:** Configure the tool to identify security vulnerabilities.
3. **Scan Your Code:** Scan your codebase. The tool will generate a report with potential issues, and recommendations.
4. **Review and Fix:** Review the code, and fix all the issues that were reported.
5. **Regular Scans:** Setup a system to scan your code base at regular intervals.

Practical Implementation: Hiring a Penetration Tester

1. **Find a Reputable Penetration Testing Company:** Look for a reputable penetration testing company, and choose an ethical hacker that has expertise with your tech stack.
2. **Agree on Scope:** Create a well defined scope of the areas that you want the security experts to test.
3. **Set up a Timeline:** Create a timeline for the tests, and for the reporting process.
4. **Receive Reports:** The ethical hacker will provide you with reports on the tests, and the vulnerabilities that were found.
5. **Address Issues:** Use the information that you received to make changes to your system to address security concerns.
6. **Retest:** If necessary, retest your system after the fixes have been applied.

Key Considerations

- **Regularity:** Perform security audits and penetration testing on a regular schedule. Security testing is not a one-time activity, it is a continuous process.
- **External Experts:** Consider hiring external experts for penetration testing, to have an unbiased perspective.
- **Prioritize Issues:** Prioritize the vulnerabilities and security issues that you have found based on their potential risk.
- **Document:** Document all security tests that have been done, and the changes that have been made.
- **Act on Results:** Always make changes, and updates based on the findings from the tests.

Personal Insights

From my experience, I have found that implementing security audits, and penetration testing are key for creating reliable, and secure enterprise applications. They are essential to ensure that your code is free from vulnerabilities, and that your applications can withstand real world attacks. These practices are essential for maintaining a strong security posture, and should be part of your development process.

Summary

Regular security audits and penetration testing are crucial components of any robust security program. By regularly testing your applications with different security testing techniques, you'll be able to identify vulnerabilities before attackers do, and protect your application from security breaches.

In the next section, we'll explore how to comply with data privacy regulations.

9.4 UNDERSTANDING AND COMPLYING WITH DATA PRIVACY REGULATIONS

In today's data-driven world, protecting user privacy is not just a legal obligation—it's a moral imperative. As developers, we have a responsibility to handle user data with the utmost care and respect. Data privacy regulations such as GDPR (General Data Protection Regulation) and CCPA (California Consumer Privacy Act) provide a framework for how we should collect, process, and store user data. These regulations are not just a set of legal requirements, they represent ethical guidelines for responsible data handling.

In this section, we'll explore the key aspects of data privacy regulations, why compliance is crucial, and how you can implement these principles in your Next.js 15 applications. Think of this section as becoming a guardian of your users' privacy and building applications that are not only functional but also respectful of user rights.

Why Are Data Privacy Regulations Important?

- **User Protection:** Regulations such as GDPR and CCPA protect user's data from being collected, processed, and used without their consent.
- **Legal Compliance:** They are legally required, and non-compliance can result in hefty fines, and legal actions.
- **User Trust:** Users trust companies that handle their data with respect and transparency.
- **Brand Reputation:** Data breaches can have a negative impact on a company's brand, and result in a loss of user trust.
- **Ethical Responsibility:** As developers, it is our ethical responsibility to protect user data.

In short, understanding and complying with data privacy regulations is a must for building trustworthy and reliable applications.

Key Concepts of Data Privacy Regulations

Let's explore some of the key concepts of data privacy regulations:

1. **Consent:**
   - **What it is:** Obtaining explicit consent before collecting, processing, or storing any personal data.
   - **Best Practices:** Provide clear, and concise information about what data you collect, and how you plan on using it. Make sure that the user has actively given consent.
2. **Data Minimization:**
   - **What it is:** Collecting only the minimal amount of data that is necessary for your application to function correctly.
   - **Best Practices:** Only request what is needed. Avoid collecting unnecessary information.
3. **Purpose Limitation:**
   - **What it is:** Only use the collected data for the purpose that was explicitly specified to the user.
   - **Best Practices:** Do not use the collected information for anything that was not clearly communicated to your users.
4. **Transparency:**
   - **What it is:** Providing clear and easy-to-understand information about how your application is handling user data.
   - **Best Practices:** Provide a privacy policy that details what data you are collecting, why you are collecting it, and how you are protecting it.
5. **Data Security:**

- o **What it is:** Implementing strong security measures to protect user data from unauthorized access.
- o **Best Practices:** Use secure coding practices, secure storage methods, and implement strong authentication, and authorization.

6. **User Rights:**
   - o **What it is:** Granting users the rights to access, modify, delete, or transfer their personal data.
   - o **Best Practices:** Provide a clear and easy way to access, modify, or delete their data.
7. **Data Retention:**
   - o **What it is:** Only retain user data for as long as it is needed.
   - o **Best Practices:** Delete data when it is not needed anymore, and implement a data retention policy.

Practical Implementation in a Next.js 15 Application

Let's explore a few practical examples:

1. **Consent Management:**
   - o Show a consent banner before collecting any user data, and store the consent preferences in the user's session.
   - o Make sure you have an opt-in consent instead of an opt-out consent.
2. **Implementing Data Minimization:**
   - o Only collect the data you absolutely need.
   - o If you are loading data from an API, load only the data that you need, and ignore the fields that are not needed.
3. **Implementing Transparency:**
   - o Create a privacy policy that details what data you are collecting, why you are collecting it, and who you are sharing it with.
   - o Provide a clear and easy way to access your privacy policy.
4. **Implementing User Rights:**
   - o Create settings pages where users can access, modify, or delete their data.
   - o Make sure that the user has a way to export their data.
5. **Data Security Practices:**
   - o As we discussed in previous chapters, always use secure coding practices, encrypt data, and use secure storage methods for API keys, and secrets.

Key Considerations

- **Consult Legal Experts:** Always seek legal advice when setting up your application's data privacy mechanisms.
- **Be Transparent:** Be transparent with your users on what data you are collecting, and how you are using it.
- **Regularly Review:** Review your policies to ensure compliance with changing regulations.
- **Train Your Team:** Train your development team on how to handle user data, and make sure they are aware of your policies.
- **Document Everything:** Always document how your application is handling personal data.

Personal Insights

From my experience, I have learned that data privacy should be a major concern for all developers. I always recommend creating a privacy policy from the beginning of a project, and always being transparent with your users on how you are handling their data. You must always take a user-centric approach, and prioritize the user's privacy, and security. As a developer, I see this as a way of gaining the trust of my users, and creating a positive relationship with them.

Summary

By understanding and complying with data privacy regulations, you'll be able to build applications that are not only functional but also ethical and trustworthy. Remember that handling data correctly and transparently is not just a legal requirement, it is the right thing to do.

In the next chapter, we'll discuss strategies for continuous improvement, and the future of Next.js

CHAPTER 10: CONTINUOUS IMPROVEMENT AND THE FUTURE

Alright, we've reached the final chapter of our journey. We've covered the core concepts of Next.js 15, explored architectural patterns, delved into security, and optimized performance. But building great applications is not a one-time task, it's a continuous process of learning, iterating, and adapting. This chapter is all about how to maintain, improve, and look towards the future of your applications.

In this chapter, we'll explore techniques for refactoring, and maintaining your codebase. We will discuss the importance of A/B testing and experimentation, how to iterate on your application features, and provide some insights into the future of Next.js in the enterprise. This chapter will be your guide to building applications that not only work but also constantly evolve, improve, and adapt to changing requirements.

10.1 REFACTORING AND MAINTAINING NEXT.JS APPLICATIONS

In the world of software development, especially in enterprise settings, building an application is just the beginning. The real challenge lies in maintaining it over time, adapting to changing requirements, and ensuring it remains robust and performant. Refactoring is an essential part of this process. It is like renovating your house; by refactoring your application, you keep it modern, flexible, and easy to manage. It is also essential to understand that an application does not stay the same over time. Your user's needs will change, and the business will change, and your code must be able to keep up with the changes.

In this section, we'll explore why refactoring and maintenance are crucial, common refactoring techniques, and best practices for keeping your Next.js 15 applications healthy and scalable. Think of this as setting up a continuous improvement process for your application, ensuring it remains top-notch even as time passes.

Why Are Refactoring and Maintenance Important?

- **Prevent Technical Debt:** Over time, code can accumulate technical debt, leading to slow development cycles, and bugs. Refactoring keeps your code organized.
- **Improved Code Quality:** Improves the internal structure, and readability of your code, without changing its external behavior.
- **Increased Maintainability:** By making the code cleaner, it is easier to make changes, fix bugs, and add new features, which improves maintainability, and reduces the overall cost.
- **Reduced Bugs:** Refactoring improves code, making it more testable, and less likely to have bugs.
- **Improved Performance:** Refactoring code and database logic might improve the application's performance.
- **Adopting New Technologies:** Refactoring makes it easier to adopt new technologies as you are simplifying your code base, and refactoring helps you move code to more modern approaches.
- **Long Term Success:** Refactoring is crucial for the long term success of your application.

In short, refactoring and maintenance are essential for building applications that can withstand the test of time.

Common Refactoring Techniques

Let's explore some common refactoring techniques that you can use:

1. **Code Cleanup and Reorganization:**
   - **How it works:** Cleaning and reorganizing code, moving code to the correct folder, removing unused code, formatting code, and making sure everything is well organized.
   - **Best Practices:** Use tools like ESLint and Prettier to enforce code style and standards.
2. **Component Extraction:**
   - **How it works:** Extracting reusable components from larger components to make your code more modular, and easier to reuse.
   - **Best Practices:** Create reusable components that can be used in different parts of the application.
3. **Function Extraction:**
   - **How it works:** Extracting smaller functions from bigger functions, to create single purpose and testable units.
   - **Best Practices:** Create small, testable functions that perform specific tasks. This also increases readability of the code.

4. **Code Simplification:**
   - **How it works:** Refactoring overly complicated functions by reducing the complexity of the code.
   - **Best Practices:** Simplify logic and algorithms. Use smaller functions that are easier to test, and understand.
5. **Database Optimizations:**
   - **How It Works:** Optimizing database queries, indexes, and database interactions.
   - **Best Practices:** Normalize your data, use appropriate indexes, and optimize your database queries.
6. **Data Normalization:**
   - **How it works:** As mentioned in previous sections, always normalize your data, transforming it to match the format you need in your UI.
   - **Best Practices:** You should always normalize data you receive from the server to match the shape that your components expect.
7. **Removing Dead Code:**
   - **How it works:** Removing code that is not used anymore from your code base, reducing bundle size.
   - **Best Practices:** You should regularly scan your code base to remove unused code.
8. **Dependency Management:**
   - **How It Works:** Evaluate the libraries that you use, and upgrade them if needed. If you find a dependency that is no longer needed, you should remove it to prevent increasing the size of your application bundle.
   - **Best Practices:** Always check if your dependencies are up to date. Always remove libraries that are not needed.
9. **Improving Performance:**
   - **How It Works:** Implement lazy loading, code splitting, optimize images, and use all the performance best practices that we have covered in previous chapters.
10. **Automated Testing:**
    - **How It Works:** Implement unit tests, integration tests, and end-to-end tests.
    - **Best Practices:** Aim for a high test coverage. All changes that you make should be covered by automated tests.

Practical Implementation: Refactoring a Component

Let's see how we can refactor a component to make it more readable.

1. **Original component (src/app/components/ProductCard.tsx)**:

```
    interface ProductProps {
  id: string
  name: string
  description: string
  price: number
   imageUrl: string
 }


const ProductCard: React.FC<ProductProps> = ({id, name,
description, price, imageUrl}) => {
  return (
      <div className="border p-4">
          <img src={imageUrl} alt={name} className="w-32 h-
32 object-cover"/>
          <h2>{name}</h2>
          <p>{description}</p>
          <p>Price: ${price}</p>
          <button onClick={() => console.log('Add to cart',
id)}>Add to cart</button>
      </div>
  )
 }
export default ProductCard
```

This component has all the logic mixed together.

2. **Refactor this component to create smaller, reusable components**:
   o Create a new component to handle the image
     src/app/components/ProductImage.tsx:

```
    interface ProductImageProps {
 imageUrl: string
  alt: string



}
```

```
      const ProductImage: React.FC<ProductImageProps> =
({imageUrl, alt}) => {
  return (
      <img src={imageUrl} alt={alt} className="w-32 h-32
object-cover"/>
    )
 }
export default ProductImage
```

- o Create a new component to handle the add to cart button
  src/app/components/AddToCartButton.tsx:

```
      interface AddToCartButtonProps {
 id: string
}


const AddToCartButton: React.FC<AddToCartButtonProps> =
({id}) => {
    return (
     <button onClick={() => console.log('Add to cart',
id)}>Add to cart</button>
    )
 }
export default AddToCartButton
```

- o Update the ProductCard to use this components
  src/app/components/ProductCard.tsx:

```
      import AddToCartButton from "./AddToCartButton";
import ProductImage from "./ProductImage";

  interface ProductProps {
     id: string
     name: string
     description: string
     price: number
```

```
    imageUrl: string

  }


const ProductCard: React.FC<ProductProps> = ({id, name,
description, price, imageUrl}) => {
    return (
        <div className="border p-4">
          <ProductImage imageUrl={imageUrl} alt={name} />
           <h2>{name}</h2>
          <p>{description}</p>
          <p>Price: ${price}</p>
            <AddToCartButton id={id} />
        </div>

    )

  }
export default ProductCard
```

By implementing this refactoring we have created components that are easier to maintain, and reuse, and the main ProductCard component is much more clear.

Key Considerations

- **Refactor Incrementally:** Refactor code in small steps. Avoid refactoring large sections of code at once.
- **Test:** Always test after a refactor to make sure nothing was broken.
- **Code Reviews:** Implement code reviews, to ensure that the code is refactored correctly.
- **Document:** Document all code changes, and the reasoning for the refactor.

Personal Insights

From my experience, refactoring is not just about making code look pretty; it is also about making your application easier to maintain, extend, and debug. Always be on the lookout for opportunities to improve your code, but also remember that you should not over-engineer your code. I have always preferred to refactor small sections of code at a time, instead of refactoring a large module, as that reduces the chance of introducing bugs.

Summary

By implementing refactoring best practices, you'll ensure that your Next.js 15 application remains easy to maintain, extend, and adapt to changing requirements. By keeping your code base organized, and easy to understand, you will be able to maintain it for the years to come.

In the next section, we'll explore A/B testing and experimentation strategies.

10.2 A/B TESTING AND EXPERIMENTATION STRATEGIES

In the ever-evolving landscape of web development, making informed decisions about your application's features is paramount. You can't just rely on intuition or assumptions. That's where A/B testing and experimentation strategies become indispensable. They allow you to test different ideas, validate hypotheses, and make data-driven decisions about how to improve your application. It's about creating a system that allows you to learn from your users, and create a better product.

In this section, we'll explore what A/B testing and experimentation are, why they are crucial for application development, and how you can implement them effectively in your Next.js 15 applications. Think of this section as creating a laboratory for your application, where you can try different approaches, measure their results, and learn from your experiments.

Why Are A/B Testing and Experimentation Important?

- **Data-Driven Decisions:** They help in making informed decisions based on data instead of assumptions, which results in better outcomes.
- **User-Centric Approach:** Allows you to optimize your application for your user's behavior, resulting in higher engagement.
- **Reduced Risk:** Reduces the risk of launching new features that do not work well.

- **Improved Conversion Rates:** A/B testing helps you identify the features that work best, and the user flows that work better, which increases conversion rates.
- **Continuous Improvement:** Enables a continuous improvement process by allowing you to iterate and make incremental changes based on data.
- **Reduced Bounce Rates:** By improving your user experience with A/B testing, you will be able to reduce bounce rates.

In short, A/B testing and experimentation are crucial for building successful, user-centric applications, that are constantly being optimized for your users.

Understanding A/B Testing

A/B testing (also called split testing) is a method for comparing two versions of a web page, app, or any other digital product to determine which version performs better. The goal is to measure the impact of a specific change on user behavior. A/B testing will give you data that will inform what is the most successful way of designing a specific feature, or page.

- **How It Works:** Users are randomly divided into two or more groups: each group is presented with a different version, and you measure the user's engagement using specific metrics.
- **Objective:** Identify the best version by measuring its impact using metrics, and analytics.
- **Metrics:** Common metrics are: Conversion rates, engagement, and bounce rates.

Understanding Experimentation

Experimentation goes beyond A/B testing. It involves a more holistic approach to validating different ideas by using data and scientific methods. Experimentation is often used when testing multiple variations, or trying completely new approaches to a problem.

- **How It Works:** You define a hypothesis, implement experiments, analyze data, and iterate based on the results.
- **Objective:** To learn what works best, and make better decisions.
- **Methods:** Involves A/B tests, multivariate tests, user behavior analysis, surveys, and other ways of understanding your users behavior.

A/B Testing vs. Experimentation

While A/B testing is a specific technique, experimentation is the overall process of testing and validating assumptions using a variety of methods. A/B testing is used to test a specific change, while experimentation is a more general way of testing ideas, using data, and making informed decisions.

Practical Implementation in Next.js 15

Let's explore a few examples of how to implement A/B testing and experimentation in your application:

1. **Setting up an A/B Testing Tool:** You can use tools such as Google Optimize, Optimizely, VWO, or LaunchDarkly. These tools will handle most of the logic required for A/B testing.
2. **Defining Your Experiment:** Define the hypothesis you want to test. For example, you might want to test if changing the color of a button will lead to more engagement.
3. **Creating Variations:** Create two versions of your component, where you will be testing a particular change.
4. **Implementing A/B testing:** Use the code that your A/B testing tool will provide you, and wrap your component with the code that will show one variation, or the other based on your configurations.
5. **Tracking Metrics:** Define the metrics that you want to use to analyze your results. Examples include: Button clicks, engagement time, or conversion rates.

Practical Implementation using Google Optimize:

1. **Create Google Optimize Account:** Go to optimize.google.com and create an account.
2. **Create an Experiment:** Create a new experiment, and define the goal, and the different variations.
3. **Install Google Analytics:** You will also need Google Analytics on your website.
4. **Get the Code:** Google Optimize will give you the necessary code for the A/B testing that you want to create.
5. **Implement Google Optimize Code in Next.js:** In src/app/layout.tsx add the code provided by Google Optimize for your experiment:

```
'use client';
import "./globals.css";
```

```
import type { Metadata } from "next";
import Header from "./components/Header";
import Footer from "./components/Footer";
 import { useEffect } from "react";

export const metadata: Metadata = {
    title: "My Enterprise App",
    description: "The best app ever",
};

export default function RootLayout({
    children,
}: {
    children: React.ReactNode;
}) {

  useEffect(() => {
    if (typeof window !== 'undefined') {
      // Add google optimize code here.

(function(i,s,o,g,r,a,m){i['GoogleAnalyticsObject']=r;i[r]=i[
r]||function(){
            (i[r].q=i[r].q||[]).push(arguments)},i[r].l=1*new
Date();a=s.createElement(o),

m=s.getElementsByTagName(o)[0];a.async=1;a.src=g;m.parentNode
.insertBefore(a,m)
      })(window,document,'script','https://www.google-
analytics.com/analytics.js','ga');

      window.ga('create', 'YOUR_GOOGLE_ANALYTICS_ID',
'auto');
      window.ga('send', 'pageview');


      (function(a,s,y,n,c,h,i,d,e){s.className+='
'+y;h.start=1*new Date;

h.end=i=function(){s.className=s.className.replace(RegExp('
?'+y),'')};
```

```
(a[n]=a[n]||[]).hide=h;setTimeout(function(){i()},c);h.end(d,
e);})(window,
        document.documentElement,'async-hide','dataLayer',400,
        {'YOUR_GOOGLE_OPTIMIZE_ID':true},
        null,null,null,null);
    }
    }, []);



    return (
        <html lang="en">
          <body>
            <Header/>
            {children}
            <Footer />
          </body>
        </html>
    );
}
```

Replace YOUR_GOOGLE_ANALYTICS_ID with your Google
Analytics ID, and YOUR_GOOGLE_OPTIMIZE_ID with your
Google Optimize ID.

6. **Implement the A/B testing code:** In the components where you
   want to run the A/B test, you need to add the code that is generated
   by Google Optimize.
7. **Analyze results:** Google Optimize has a dashboard that you can use
   to analyze the results, based on the goal, and the metrics that you
   have defined.

Key Considerations

- **Define Clear Goals:** Define the goal for each experiment, and create
  clear metrics.
- **Start Small:** Test one variable at a time, and do not run too many
  experiments at the same time.

- **Use a Control Group:** Always have a control group where you are not making any changes.
- **Test Thoroughly:** Do not make assumptions about the results, always test your hypotheses, and make data driven decisions.
- **Iterate:** Use the results of your experiments to improve your application, and create new experiments based on the results you are obtaining.

Personal Insights

From my experiences, A/B testing and experimentation are critical for building products that users love. They are essential for making data-driven decisions about the future of your application. I have been involved in projects where decisions were made based on assumptions, and those decisions were not the right ones. By using A/B testing we were able to understand what features resonated best with our users. I always encourage teams to experiment, and test everything, and make changes based on real data, and not just assumptions.

Summary

A/B testing and experimentation should be an essential part of your development process, as they allow you to build data driven and user centric applications. By using these practices, you will continuously improve your application, and create a much better experience for your users.

In the next section, we will explore how to iterate on your application's features and performance, based on the data that you have collected.

10.3 ITERATING ON APPLICATION FEATURES AND PERFORMANCE

In the dynamic world of software development, building a great application is not a one-time event; it's a continuous journey of improvement and adaptation. You don't just launch a new feature and forget about it. You should always be monitoring user feedback, analyzing usage patterns, and optimizing your code for peak performance. This is where iteration becomes so crucial. Iteration is a process that allows you to continuously improve your application, by making changes based on data, and feedback.

In this section, we'll explore the importance of iteration, discuss how to gather user feedback, analyze performance data, and implement changes to your application for a continuous process of improvement. Think of this section as creating a feedback loop for your application, ensuring that it's always getting better, and always meeting the ever-evolving needs of your users.

Why Is Iteration Important?

- **User Satisfaction:** Iteration ensures that your application is constantly being improved to meet your users' needs, which results in user satisfaction.
- **Performance Optimization:** Continuous monitoring and optimization ensures that your application performs well, leading to a better user experience.
- **Reduced Risk:** By continuously releasing small features and changes, the overall risk of a large failure is reduced.
- **Business Agility:** Iteration enables your application to adapt to new business requirements, and changes in user behavior.
- **Competitive Advantage:** By continuously improving your application, you will create a competitive advantage, by making sure that your application is better than the competition.
- **Better Return on Investment:** By optimizing your application to meet the user's needs, you will be able to get more return on your investment.

In short, iteration is the key to creating successful applications that stand the test of time.

Key Strategies for Iterating on Features and Performance

Let's explore the strategies that you should follow to improve your application:

1. **Gather User Feedback:**
   - **How it works:** Collect feedback from your users using different channels, such as surveys, questionnaires, interviews, contact forms, user forums, reviews, and user testing.
   - **Best Practices:** Use a variety of feedback methods, and make sure that the feedback is always received, and considered.
2. **Analyze Usage Patterns:**

- How it works: Analyze data from analytics platforms to see how your users are using your application. Use tools like Google Analytics, and other tracking tools to track usage metrics, and patterns.
- Best Practices: Focus on user behavior and pain points, to discover areas of your application that can be improved.

3. **Track Error Rates:**
   - How it works: Track your application's error rates using monitoring tools, such as Sentry, and Datadog.
   - Best Practices: Pay attention to the errors that happen in your application, and try to understand why they happen. Fix issues as soon as possible.

4. **Track Performance Metrics:**
   - How it works: Track key performance metrics such as page load times, API response times, and component rendering times, using tools like the browser dev tools, and monitoring tools.
   - Best Practices: Use performance tools to identify bottlenecks in your application, and make performance optimization changes regularly.

5. **Set Performance Budgets:**
   - How It Works: Set performance budgets for your application, including your bundle size, number of HTTP requests, image sizes, and other important performance metrics.
   - Best Practices: Always try to stay within your set performance budgets.

6. **Use A/B Testing and Experimentation:**
   - How it Works: Test different versions of a feature, to see which version performs better, using A/B testing tools.
   - Best Practices: Always test any new features that you are implementing. You can also use these techniques to experiment with new flows or layouts.

7. **Continuous Deployment:**
   - How it Works: Continuously deploy your changes to production using a CI/CD pipeline.
   - Best Practices: By continuously deploying small changes you will be able to reduce risk, and ensure that your application is always up-to-date.

8. **Regular Refactoring:**
   - How It Works: Refactor your code, database queries, and your architecture, based on new findings, and feedback.

- Best Practices: Use automated tests to ensure that refactoring does not break your code. Refactor often, do not wait until your code becomes messy.

Practical Implementation

Let's explore how to create a feedback loop in your Next.js application:

1. **Implement a Feedback Form:** Create a form that users can use to provide feedback. You can use a form component that allows you to get information from the user, including any comments, or suggestions, and allow them to rate their overall experience.
2. **Track User Interaction:** Use tools such as Google Analytics to track how users are using your application. Always track how often a component is used, what pages your users visit the most, and what user flows are more common.
3. **Track Errors:** Use monitoring tools such as Sentry or Datadog, to track errors in your application. Set up alerts to notify you of any critical errors.
4. **Analyze Data:** Analyze all the information you have gathered to identify areas of improvement in your application. Always correlate your user feedback with the usage patterns, performance data, and errors you are observing.
5. **Create Experiments:** Create A/B tests, or run experiments to validate your hypotheses. You can create new layouts, different flows, or different components, to test the best version of your features.
6. **Implement Changes:** Implement any code changes, and performance changes that you have identified.
7. **Deploy:** Use a CI/CD pipeline to deploy new versions of your application.
8. **Re-evaluate:** Re-evaluate the performance metrics, user feedback, and usage patterns, and start the process again.

Key Considerations

- **Make User Feedback a Priority:** Always listen to the users. It is their experience that should guide your decisions.
- **Be Data Driven:** Always back your decisions with data.
- **Be Agile:** Be flexible and agile, and adapt to change when necessary.
- **Prioritize Based on Impact:** Focus on the areas that will have the most impact in your application.

- **Regularly Review:** Regularly review your application's performance and user experience.

Personal Insight

From my experience, the art of building great applications is not about building perfect systems; it's about learning, adapting, and continuously improving. I encourage you to never stop looking for new ways to improve your application. Always experiment, try new things, and always be looking for opportunities to make your application faster, more reliable, and user friendly.

Summary

Iterating on your application is a must for creating successful applications. By implementing a feedback loop that gathers data from your users, performance metrics, and by experimenting and testing your hypotheses, you will be able to make continuous improvements to your application.

In the next section, we will discuss the future of Next.js in the enterprise.

10.4 THE EVOLVING LANDSCAPE OF NEXT.JS IN THE ENTERPRISE

As we conclude our journey through the world of Next.js 15, it's crucial to take a moment to look ahead and explore the evolving landscape of this powerful framework, especially within the context of enterprise applications. Next.js is not a static tool; it's constantly evolving, and it's always getting better, and more powerful, so it is key to stay up to date with its innovations, and new features.

In this section, we'll explore the key trends and emerging features that are shaping the future of Next.js in enterprise development. Think of this section as peeking into the future, understanding what the future holds for Next.js, and how it can help you create better enterprise applications in the years to come.

Key Trends Shaping the Future of Next.js

1. **Server Components as a Core Principle:**

- o **What it is:** Server components are becoming a central part of Next.js development, offering many advantages over traditional client side components.
- o **Why it matters:** They improve performance by rendering code on the server, and also they improve SEO by providing better initial load times.
- o **Impact:** Server components are simplifying the way we develop applications, by allowing server side logic directly within the same component, and we expect them to be used more and more in the future.
- o **Best practices:** By default create server components, and use client components only when needed.
2. **Streaming and Suspense for Better User Experience:**
   - o **What it is:** Streaming allows you to render your components gradually as they are being rendered on the server, which makes the user experience better by making your applications feel faster, and more interactive. Suspense helps you handle loading states, and improve the experience during the loading process.
   - o **Why it matters:** Streaming and Suspense provide a better user experience, by rendering parts of the application as soon as they are available. This leads to applications that feel faster, and more interactive.
   - o **Impact:** We expect to see more usage of Suspense and Streaming, to provide enhanced user experiences.
   - o **Best Practices:** Always implement Suspense, and explore options to use Streaming.
3. **Server Actions for Simplified Data Mutations:**
   - o **What it is:** Server actions allow you to perform server-side data mutations directly from your React components, by calling server functions from your client code.
   - o **Why it matters:** They simplify the process of creating forms, and handling data mutations, which reduces complexity, and makes your code easier to manage.
   - o **Impact:** We expect to see an increase in the usage of Server Actions in the future, as they are easier to implement, and reduce code complexity.
   - o **Best Practices:** Use Server Actions to handle forms, and any server side data mutations.
4. **Enhanced Data Fetching:**

- What it is: Next.js is always providing new ways to fetch data, with more performance, and control, such as the fetch API, and also more advanced data fetching hooks.
- Why it matters: Having more flexible options for data fetching, is always a must for a framework that aims to be a fullstack solution.
- Impact: We expect more improvements in the data fetching layer, with even more flexible, and performant options for the future.
- Best Practices: Implement the most optimized method based on your requirements.

5. **Edge Functions:**
- What it is: Edge functions allow you to run code closer to your users, by using a CDN. This reduces latency, as the response times are faster, improving the overall user experience.
- Why it matters: They improve performance by reducing latency, and providing better scalability.
- Impact: We expect edge functions to become more important, as they are key for providing globally performant applications.
- Best Practices: Use edge functions for API routes that need to be executed near the user, and for performance critical applications.

6. **Improved Tooling and DX (Developer Experience):**
- What it is: Next.js has a very active community, which is constantly improving the developer experience, with better documentation, more features, new libraries, and tools.
- Why it matters: An improved developer experience results in higher productivity, code maintainability, and it also enhances collaboration.
- Impact: We expect new tools to be released, which will help to improve the developer experience even further.
- Best Practices: Stay up-to-date with the latest tooling and documentation. Always use the latest version of Next.js.

7. **Fullstack Capabilities:**
- What it is: Next.js is becoming more and more a fullstack solution, allowing you to manage your entire application, both backend, and frontend.
- Why it matters: It simplifies development, reduces complexity, and allows you to manage both frontend and backend in the same codebase.

- o **Impact:** We expect more capabilities in the backend, and more server-side functionality to be introduced, that will make Next.js a true fullstack solution.
- o **Best Practices:** Use Next.js for all aspects of development when possible, this will reduce the overall complexity of your application.

8. **Component Libraries and Design Systems:**
   - o **What it is:** The community is always releasing better and more mature component libraries, and design systems that make it easier to create beautiful user interfaces, with consistent styles.
   - o **Why it matters:** Design systems and components libraries enhance collaboration between designers and developers, making the development process much more efficient.
   - o **Impact:** We expect more adoption of design systems and component libraries in enterprise settings, to increase developer efficiency.
   - o **Best Practices:** Implement your own component library, or adopt a third party component library or design system.

Practical Implementation:

While it is hard to showcase practical implementation of future technologies, make sure you are always up to date with the latest version of Next.js. Try to always use the new features that Next.js releases, and adapt your code base as needed, to take advantage of all that Next.js has to offer.

Personal Insight

From my experience, Next.js is one of the most exciting frameworks in the market, and it has been transforming how we build web applications. I find that the framework is continuously evolving, and it provides new and powerful tools with every release. I always recommend developers to stay up-to-date with the new versions, try all the new features, and implement them in their projects when they see a clear benefit. The key is to be always learning, and evolving with the framework.

Summary

The future of Next.js in the enterprise is looking very bright. By embracing new technologies, and adopting a mindset of continuous learning, you will be able to take advantage of all the power that Next.js has to offer, and to create amazing applications.

This marks the end of our journey! I hope this book has provided you with the right tools and best practices, to help you in your journey of building enterprise applications with Next.js. Thank you for coming on this journey with me!